The I.D. Master

Identity Change Insider Secrets
Little Known Tactics of
Identity Change Professionals

by John Q. Newman

D1452118

PALADIN PRESS
Boulder, Colorado

Certain passages in this book may reference laws in an informal and general manner. The publisher, author, and distributors of this book do not purport to be attorneys, nor do they advocate illegal activity. The information presented in this book should not be relied upon or used without first consulting an attorney and researching the applicable laws of the appropriate jurisdictions.

Some or all of the ideas presented herein may be considered illegal in many jurisdictions of the United States and elsewhere. This book is presented *for academic study only*.

The I.D. Master:
Little Known Tactics of Identity Change Professionals
by John Q. Newman

Copyright © 2002 by John Q. Newman

ISBN 10: 1-58160-519-6
ISBN 13: 978- 1-58160-519-8
Printed in the United States of America

Published by Paladin Press, a division of
Paladin Enterprises, Inc.
Gunbarrel Tech Center
7077 Winchester Circle
Boulder, Colorado 80301 USA
+1.303.443.7250

Direct inquiries and/or orders to the above address.

PALADIN, PALADIN PRESS, and the "horse head" design
are trademarks belonging to Paladin Enterprises and
registered in United States Patent and Trademark Office.

Visit our Web site at www.paladin-press.com

Contents

Introduction

The events of September 11, 2001, have dramatically changed the entire concept of identity and security in the United States. In general, the actual mechanics of identity creation and verification have not changed, but identities are screened more completely. Prior to September 11, it was still quite possible to fly on airplanes without showing identification. Although regulations technically required photo identification from passengers, this requirement was often not enforced. Also, identity documents must now be presented when picking up train tickets.

Certain types of employment are now off-limits for those operating under new identities unless these identities have been totally backstopped with the necessary documents and records. One example of this is airport workers. Anyone who works at an airport and has a security badge had better be who they say they are. Hundreds of hapless individuals have found this out in airports in Boston, Las Vegas, and Salt Lake City. The authorities ran massive sting operations on airport employees in all of these cities. The identification documents that were provided by all employees at these airports were checked. In many cases, undocumented workers from Mexico had used counterfeit green cards to obtain their employment. Ordinarily, these fake green cards are perfect, because the only agency that can verify them is the U.S. Immigration and Naturalization Service (INS). In this instance, these cards were actually verified by the agency that was supposed to have issued them, found to be false, and the workers were arrested.

The usual disposition of such cases would have resulted in quick deportation back to Mexico, but it is a reflection of the new times we live in that this did not happen. The U.S. federal government is prosecuting all of these people on federal charges, and most, if not all of them, will do at least a few months in a federal prison before they are deported.

This increased harshness illustrates why it is necessary to stay carefully informed when living under, or contemplating living under, a new identity. Over the years, I have written many books on the new-identity creation process. These books describe the fundamentals of identity changing and illustrate how to successfully penetrate the system and start over. Successful identity changing is all about paying close attention to details — failure to do so can have dire consequences. This is an endeavor where the old saying, "the devil is in the details," cannot be more true. One can read stories in the media on a regular basis of people who were caught trying to "start over" with a new set of papers.

However, there is another side to all of this. Millions of people in the United States live and work under a false identity every day. These people run the gamut from the few thousands who have received new identities courtesy of the U.S. government, to the nearly six million illegal aliens who report to work every day with fake driver's licenses, green cards, and other documents.

The economies of Southern California and South Texas would cease to function if all of these people — primarily from Mexico and Central America — were deported. Employers, landlords, and others look the other way when presented with the questionable documents frequently carried by these individuals. The problem has become so severe that a few states are now willing to issue driver's licenses to these workers so that the rapidly increasing problem of unlicensed, uninsured illegal-immigrant motorists can be eliminated. In Texas and California, some banks will now open accounts for these people with foreign identity documents.

However, the fake identities usually created by illegal immigrants will not withstand even a superficial examination. Their fake driver's licenses will not pass a computer check, and their green cards have no record in the computer. The thrust of my writings on new-identity creation has always been about how to create an identity that can safely be used and withstand scrutiny: The driver's license is real; the credit cards are not forgeries, etc.

This book is about less well-known tricks of the trade to create a new identity. Much of this information has come to me via those who are living the life and want to share anonymously their lessons from the school of hard knocks. I thank all of those who helped.

This book is not intended to be a primer on how to create a new identity. It is assumed the reader has a working knowledge of the basics. If not, I suggest the reader first obtain copies of the following books:

The Heavy Duty New Identity, Second Edition, by John Q. Newman

Reborn in the U.S.A., Third Edition, by Trent Sands

Understanding U.S. Identity Documents, by John Q. Newman

This would be a minimum reading list, and I would suggest that many more books, in addition to these, be read. All the titles mentioned in this book are listed in the Recommended Reading. These and many other titles, are available from Loompanics Unlimited at www.loompanics.com.

Some will say that books like this aid those who would do acts of destruction similar to those which occurred in New York City and Washington, D.C. It needs to be remembered that groups like the ones who carried out these deeds are already well versed in all aspects of this subject. In fact, some of the terrorists stole identities in their home countries before they arrived in America, and border control officials admitted all of them into the United States legally. The information presented in this book is only for academic interest, and the author and the publisher do not advocate or condone the violation of any laws.

Finally, be aware that the authorities are not stupid. Once a lot of people start using the methods outlined in this book, new procedures may be put into place. Always know before you go. Find out in advance what is required from the agency involved to get the document you want.

.

CHAPTER ONE

Using the Law to Create a New Identity

Most methods of identity changing are illegal. The actual identity change is not illegal, but most subsequent attempts to document that identity are. The instant you apply for a driver's license, voter registration card, or other documents under the new identity, you break a myriad of laws. The paradox of the illegal identity change is that when it is done correctly, it is all but undetectable.

A Legal Identity Change Method

A natural question is: Can one change one's identity in a legal fashion and still obtain the benefits of a clandestine identity change? The answer is both yes and no. To understand this paradox, we need to look at the benefits of the clandestine identity change.

The primary benefit of the classic "paper trip" method is that there is no connection between the old and new identity. When done correctly, the identity changer emerges as a totally redocumented person with no ties to the old self. This type of identity change is perfect for privacy hounds, fugitives, and criminals who want a second identity in order to commit new crimes. In the case of the criminal, it can be the perfect crime, because any arrest warrants issued by the police will be in the name of the false identity. If this identity has real documents behind it, the police will have no reason to even suspect that it is a phony. The criminal simply discards the fake identity once it has become "hot" and moves on.

The legal identity-change method allows the individual to change identities without breaking any laws. The drawback is that a public record will be created that links the new identity with the old. However, if done carefully, and with some added flourishes, the record can be made very obscure and next to impossible to find. Unless someone had a reason to think you had changed your name, there would be no evidence of such.

The Name-Change Laws

The legal identity-change method uses the name-change laws to your advantage. In the United States, people have a common-law right to use whatever name they want, so long as the purpose is not to evade the law, to defraud, or to avoid personal obligations. There are two recognized methods of name change in most states.

One of these is known as the "use" method. Simply stated, the person just starts using the new name in everyday business. If the person becomes generally known in the community by this name, some states will allow you to obtain new official documents in this name. In some states, a simple "declaration of name-change form," properly notarized, may suffice.

Most states require you to "legally" change your name if you wish to receive items such as a driver's license and voter registration card in your new name. In these states, you file a petition with the court for a legal name change. In most states, this is a simple formality and you will never even go to court. If no objections are raised and the court papers are duly completed, your name-change order will be issued. This order can then be used to get a new driver's license, passport, etc., in your new name.

Choosing a State

Some states are best avoided because they impose stringent requirements. These states frequently require you to complete a detailed personal-history statement for the court, which then becomes a public document. Most states will also require you to advertise your name-change request in a local newspaper of record. In this case, it is always best to pick the local legal gazette, as few members of the public ever see this.

You will need to satisfy the residency requirement. This requirement will vary from state to state. In some locales it may be as little as six weeks, in others it may be six months or longer. Proof of residency can be established by voter registration, lease agreements, etc. More often than not, the applicant simply attests in the petition to the fact that they have met the residency requirement. Some states require that a witness who has known the applicant sign a notarized statement to the fact and submit this with the petition.

How can the legal identity-change method be exploited to yield most of the benefits of a clandestine one? First, pick a state that makes name changes as easy as possible. Appendix 2 lists states where name changes are easier and Appendix 1 includes sample name change documents to illustrate what is required.

Pick a state far away from where you will reside under the new name. This ensures that there is little chance of anyone being aware of your name change where you will begin your new life. On the other hand, if this is not an issue for you, you could change your name in your present state of residence.

Most states have legal supply stores that sell complete packs with all of the forms needed to effect name changes in that particular county. I recommend that a legal typing and filing service be used.

These services will professionally type the paperwork for you and take care of the filing. This ensures that no errors are made, and the service will call you when the court order has been granted.

Obtaining Documents in the New Name

Once you have the court order of name change, you can now create your new identity. You can register to vote under your new name and you can go to the motor vehicle department and obtain a new driver's license or state identification card. You will need the name-change order and a certified copy of your original birth certificate.

If the ultimate goal is to obtain new documents that have no link to the old, it is most advantageous to obtain only a state identification card in the new name. The reason for this is that you can then go to another state and apply for a driver's license in the new name, showing this card as identification. You have never had a license in this name, and when you are asked if you already have a license, you can honestly answer "no." The other reason this is advantageous is that if you surrender an out-of-state license in your new name to obtain a new license, there is now a link between your old name and new name in the last state, which can be used to connect the two together.

The next natural question is about a new Social Security number to go with your new name. Unfortunately, if you go to the Social Security Administration with your name-change order, they will simply issue you a new Social Security card with your new name, but under the same number. This does no good, because you will now create a link with the old name that can be spotted by credit bureaus, check verification services, and others whose databases use the Social Security number as a file retrieval tool. Is it possible to get a new Social Security number to go with the new name? In Chapter Three we will examine some possible solutions to this problem.

Creating a New Identity as a Crime Victim

The police can actually help you create a new identity. Don't believe it? Neither did I until I heard about this little-known method and checked it out. This method has been successfully used by con men to easily create new identities for decades. Before we get into the details, let us take a little vacation to the Caribbean.

A few years back a rash of tourist robberies took place all over the U.S. Virgin Islands. Visitors were routinely robbed of valuables, and not just those staying in budget accommodations. Rooms in upscale hotels and resorts were also burglarized on a regular basis. One family from Toronto, Canada, had all of their money and identification stolen while they were poolside at their luxury hotel. They returned to Canada with only the shirts on their backs. What identification did they show to Canadian Customs and Immigration at the airport? The police report from the Virgin Islands police department.

These people were legitimate crime victims, but it is possible to use this as a method to start a new identity. It requires, however, the ability to be a convincing actor with law enforcement officials, and extreme attention to detail. In a nutshell, this method of identity creation revolves around obtaining a police report that says you have been the victim of a robbery in which your personal identification was stolen. The police report is then used as the centerpiece to obtain new identity documents.

The plan has two distinct phases. Phase one is getting the police report and phase two is using the police report to obtain new identification in the desired name.

Phase One: Getting the Police Report

The particulars of the identity you want to create must be learned backwards and forwards. This is particularly true in this instance, because you will have no documents to present to refresh your memory when you are asked to cough up details by the police officer. Nothing will arouse suspicion faster in the mind of the officer than if you are inconsistent about your details.

The particulars you need to learn cold will include far more than just name and birth date. The list below must be burned into your memory before you make any contact with a law enforcement officer.

- □ full name
- □ birth date
- □ birthplace
- □ marital status
- □ home address
- □ home telephone
- □ work telephone
- □ contact person
- □ signature

The object is to make it seem as if you are a tourist visiting from a distant state who has had your wallet stolen. The theft should have occurred at a public place, such as an amusement park or beach that is frequented by tourists and locals. This is very important, because it means that incidents like yours are not uncommon, and the constant crowds mean that the lack of witnesses will not seem out of the ordinary. Think about this: When was the last time you noticed a pickpocket at an amusement park?

You want to pick a major attraction in a larger city. This ensures that your case will be handled pro forma. That is, the officer will say he is sorry, take the report, give you a copy, and tell you, that unfortunately, this happens all the time, and without any witnesses or a description of the thief, there will be no investigation. The last thing you want to do is to make this report at a small town county fair, because the police department or sheriff would not have much else to do, and would treat your case as a real priority and actually investigate. You want your police report to get buried very quickly in the paperwork files, never to see the light of day again.

Preparing the Scenario. The amount of preparation this scheme will require cannot be overestimated. Every aspect of the plan must be appropriately backstopped in great detail. Consider the details involved in establishing yourself with credibility as a tourist. A tourist from far away will stay at a local hotel. This hotel should have been booked and paid for under the name and identity you wish to assume. This can cause a problem because many less expensive hotels will require photo identification when booking a room.

You can purchase a fake identity card in the name you want, but this can create a potential pitfall if the hotel does not simply look at the identification, but also writes down the ID details, or worse, makes a photocopy of the identification. Normally this detail would not be so critical, but remember, this method involves using law enforcement personnel. The last thing you want to happen is for the cop who takes the report to know that the particular hotel you are staying at makes a photocopy of the ID, and to complete his report, calls the hotel to get the license number of the bogus document. He will check it, find out it is a phony, and then come and arrest you. Remember, filing a false report, which is what this is, is a crime nearly everywhere.

There are two ways around this. The best method is to stay at a nicer hotel, paying with a credit card in the name of your intended assumed identity. Obtaining a credit card in your desired name is simple using the Visa Buxx system. The Visa Buxx card is a preloaded Visa card that can be reloaded from time to time from a bank account or another credit card. Because it is not a credit card, no credit history is required, and the card can be used at all locations where any other Visa card is accepted. Complete information on this program can be found at: www.VisaBuxx.com. The second strategy would be to pretend there are "two" people traveling, and have the name of the person checking in — your real identity — and the name of your assumed identity, both listed on the registration for the room.

Another reason for avoiding cheap motels when using this method is for simple credibility. Your story sounds a lot more plausible coming from someone staying at the Hilton or Holiday Inn than from the Fleabag Inn.

Creating Your Persona. You want to present a nice, conservative image — no long hair or unconventional attire. You want to look like a typical tourist visiting the attractions. If you are pulling this scam in Orlando, Florida, look like someone who would be visiting DisneyWorld. If you are doing this in Los Angeles, look like you are one of the legions of tourists who are seeing the sights at Universal Studios. This also extends to staying at a hotel frequented by tourists at one of these attractions. One way to cover all of these bases neatly is to book a package tour to one of these or another destination. This way, you will have tickets, hotel reservations, and other minutiae already in your assumed name. Frequently this will obviate the need to show ID at hotel check-in because the tour company will handle check-in of its guests at the hotel.

Careful thought needs to be given to your background. You will want to make yourself a resident of a far away state or even Canada. Never make yourself a resident of the same state where you pull the scam. The reason for this is that the officer taking the report, in an attempt to help you, may uncover your plan unwittingly.

If you pull this scheme in California and you tell the officer you are from California, he might try to get your driver's license number from the California DMV to put on your paperwork, so you can more rapidly obtain a duplicate driver's license from the motor vehicle department. He can readily search his own state's motor vehicle files for your license by name, whereas he will not attempt to do this if you tell him you are from Maine or Canada.

Next, make sure you are familiar with your "home" state. You will arouse suspicion if you tell the cop you are from Wisconsin, and just your luck, so is he, but you cannot answer the simplest of questions about your home town or state, and you seem to have no familiarity with anything from Wisconsin. In the age of the Internet, there is simply no reason for not doing your homework. You can get a wealth of current information on any place by reading out-of-state newspapers online, and also going to state and city tourist bureaus online and ordering their brochures.

I cautioned you to remember that police officers are not stupid. Unlike bureaucrats in ID offices, who will comply with your requests if everything is in order, police officers develop a sixth sense to know if a story is genuine or not. They must have this intuition as a requirement of doing their jobs. Cops have to make life-or-death determinations in an instant, and if your story doesn't hang together, you stand a good chance of being caught.

Once you have determined these aspects of the plan, you need to practice telling your story. It needs to sound convincing, with the right amount of anger and despair. Anger that some low-down jerk stole your wallet and ruined your vacation, and despair over what you should do next. The details need to be consistent. Map out where you want to say that your wallet was probably stolen, and what was inside of it. Make sure this part of the story is accurate and does not vary. You want your regurgitation to be accurate, but not sound rehearsed or practiced. The good news is that once the police officer has bought your story, his attitude will shift to one of protector. He will offer you compassion, be angry that it happened to you, complete the report, and tell you what to do.

In some places you will get a bonus with the police report. The officer may refer you to a crime victims' organization, which may provide you with an additional letter you can use when going to get new identification.

Phase Two: Crime Victim to a New Identity

You now have the all-important paperwork from the police department and possibly also from a crime victims' organization. The next step is turning this paperwork into the beginnings of a new identity. This can be achieved via two methods. One method involves using just the police report as the basis for obtaining new identity documents. An alternative method combines the police report with more conventional methods of identity changing. Each method has some specific benefits and possible complications.

Using the Police Report Only. The advantage of using the police report as the sole basis for obtaining new identity documents is that you will not have to present any forged instruments — birth certificates, baptismal papers, etc. — when you attempt to get a new identity. Your police report is genuine and it can be verified with a simple telephone call to the officer who wrote it. The police officer who makes the report will give you his business card, and you should make a point of presenting this to the bureaucrat at the motor vehicle department.

Your general strategy should be as follows: You are a tourist from a far away state, and your identification has been stolen. This is validated by official, verifiable paperwork from the local police or county sheriff's department. Your story at the motor vehicle department will be that you need to get a piece of photo identification right away so that you can make your trip back home. This is where the increased screening requirements for plane travel can help you obtain your new identity. You can tell the clerk at the counter that you must get some sort of photo identification or you might not be able to make your flight back home.

This is where one must pay close attention to detail. You do not attempt to obtain a driver's license. This could raise suspicion. What you urgently need, because you were robbed, is a state identification card. If they ask if you had a license from your home state, say "no." You could have a story about how you were injured in a car accident years ago and have never driven. A cane can be helpful with this.

All states have various identification requirements for issuing their documents, but they also have the ability to make exceptions in cases such as yours, in which you have documentation as a crime victim. Many states will be able to issue you a new identification card solely on your birth certificate. This may seem to defeat the purpose of this method of creating a new identity, but in fact, it dovetails with the second way of using the police report to establish a new identity.

Police Report and Birth Certificate. In some states, the motor vehicle clerk will say something to the effect of "I would really like to help you, but I need a copy of your birth certificate as well. If you can come back with both your birth certificate and the police report, it will be no problem. I am really sorry about making you have to do this after being robbed, but it is a state law." Believe it or not, this should be music to your ears. Why? Because it means if you come back with a credible counterfeit birth certificate, it will be accepted at face value with little or no scrutiny, because you have a police report.

This is the real benefit of this method. The ability to produce high-quality counterfeit birth certificates is easily within the means of most identity changers. Numerous books — including my own, *The ID Forger* — explain how to do this. So you would prepare, in advance, a birth certificate to be used when you execute the new-identity plan. But once again, you need to pay close attention to detail. If the clerk says that you must get a copy of your birth certificate, you will need to do so quickly. When you return to the office the next day or the day after, you will want to have it seem as if you had your new birth certificate express-mailed to you, either from someone "back home" or from the state vital statistics bureau. You will want to come into the office with evidence of this.

Arrange to mail a copy of your birth certificate to yourself at the hotel. This can be done via Express Mail, Federal Express, or UPS. The advantage of the last two options is that you can fill out the air bill with the appropriate return address, drop it in a local drop box, and the next day your certificate will be delivered to your hotel in a FedEx/UPS envelope. You bring the certificate to the motor vehicle office in this envelope when you return. This adds further credibility to your story.

The fact is, this is a regular occurrence, and if all of these bases are covered, and you prepare well, you will have few problems. There are a few other considerations that should be kept in mind. Some states require that all drivers' license applicants have a Social Security number, and they verify the number online to make sure it matches the name of the applicant. States such as these should be avoided. You can determine if a state does this by calling or checking at the state's web site, under motor vehicles. Nearly all states have their motor vehicle departments online. If you call, you could even explain what your situation is and find out what the particular requirements will be. In later chapters, we will examine some of the new controls in place after the terrorist attacks

(Chapter 13), and also ways to deal with the requirement to produce or provide a Social Security number (Chapter 3).

CHAPTER TWO

New Identities, The Police, and Fugitives

Many users of new identities are people who, for one reason or another, become fugitives from justice. These people run the gamut from individuals wanted for local traffic warrants or other minor crimes, to those being sought for murder and armed robbery. The media frequently carries stories of fugitives who are caught by law enforcement after having been free for many years. Anyone contemplating using a new identity because of problems with the law needs to understand how law enforcement agencies search for fugitives, and what steps they must take with their new identity to avoid capture.

Not all fugitives are created equal. No massive search is mounted for people who are wanted for traffic warrants or other relatively minor infractions. No dragnet is mounted for disorderly conduct, minor assaults, or most nonviolent crimes, unless the monetary loss was considerable. On the other hand, a real effort is made to locate people who are fugitives because of murder, armed robbery, sexual assault, major drug crimes, and nonviolent offenses where the dollar amount lost is large.

How do police go about searching for someone? Initially, when a crime is first committed, responding officers attempt to apprehend the suspect. If they are unable to locate the suspect in a few hours, the case is turned over to detectives. Detectives will then talk to the victim and other witnesses. They will also contact friends, relatives, and other known associates of the suspect in an attempt to apprehend him. Sometimes, detectives will stake out a known hangout of the suspect, hoping he will show. But this can only go on for so long. After a while, more recent cases must be investigated. At this point the case will be assigned to a fugitive recovery unit.

The U.S. Marshals and the NCIC

In the United States, the agency with primary responsibility for the apprehension of interstate fugitives is the U.S. Marshals service. They work around the country with local police and state police departments. In many jurisdictions, they form multi-agency teams who actively seek known fugitives in the area. The U.S. Marshals should never be underestimated, especially if you are wanted for serious offenses or federal crimes. Fugitive apprehension is not just a sideline for them; it is their primary reason for being.

Police agencies use a number of computer systems to help them locate fugitives. The most important one is the National Crime Information Center (NCIC). The NCIC is the fugitive's biggest enemy, because it makes a warrant issued anywhere in the country instantly available to cops everywhere.

The NCIC has numerous databases including the wanted persons index. Anytime a warrant is issued for a serious misdemeanor or felony, it is also placed on the NCIC system. The only warrants that do not get listed here are for minor, nonextradictable offenses. These are offenses where the state will not pay to have you held in another state and returned for trial in the jurisdiction where the warrant was filed. Warrants for minor driving offenses, being drunk and disorderly, etc., will not normally be posted on NCIC, only on local or statewide computers.

When the police stop an out-of-state individual during a routine traffic stop, the name and birthdate is run against the NCIC wanted person index. If a tentative hit is made, the officer calls up the rest of the warrant file to make sure that other items such as height, weight, hair color, sex, and race match. This is done because people with common names could be falsely arrested and sue. Over 600,000 arrest warrants are listed on NCIC at any one time.

For less serious offenses, a listing on NCIC can be the extent of the "search" for an individual. The police know that most fugitives will be caught if they just wait. They also know most fugitives do not go to the trouble of changing their identity. Fugitives wanted for more serious crimes, like murder, armed robbery, sexual assault, and fraud over $100,000, will be subjected to a more intensive search.

The Relative Pitfall

The marshals will compile a file of all of the suspect's relatives, their telephone numbers and addresses, and other useful biographic data. They will be particularly interested if the suspect has any brothers or sisters close to his age that he could use for a second identity. The following example is illustrative.

A few years back a woman who had been the treasurer of a small town was discovered to have embezzled hundreds of thousands of dollars. She disappeared without a trace, and even her own family had no idea where she was. A few months later, the authorities arrested her in Texas. How did they find her? It turned out she had borrowed her sister's identity without her knowledge. She had written away for a duplicate birth certificate, and with this had obtained a replacement copy of her sister's Social Security card. With this documentation, she went to Texas and got a Texas driver's license and started her life over.

The marshals have seen this ploy many times. When they investigated this woman, they ran a fifty-state search for new driver's licenses in the name of her sister. Since her sister had never lived in Texas, it made no sense when the Marshals discovered a license for her in Texas. They knew right away that the search was over.

If the marshals believe your family and friends are helping you stay on the lam, they will get telephone taps and mail covers of their incoming mail. Many fugitives are caught this way. If the fugitive has wire transfers sent to him by relatives, they can also be detected this way. The same is true if a relative allows the fugitive to use one of their credit cards to pay expenses. In short, if the Marshals believe your family is assisting you, they will place surveillance on them to locate you.

Marshals will also make note of birthdays and major holidays, and just might make a swing by your parents' or sister's house at those times to see if you show up. It sounds laughable, but each holiday season many fugitives are rounded up this way.

Marshals will also make a list of places they might think you have gone. This list will be compiled from discussions with relatives, friends, former colleagues, etc. If you always told someone that you would decamp to Honolulu if you got a chance, rest assured that the Marshals will notify their Honolulu office and the local police will be provided with a circular about you. If you bought airplane tickets to a destination a few months before you disappeared, they will learn this as well, and look for you there.

Cutting the Link Between Old and New

The key to survival for the fugitive new-identity seeker is to create a new identity, which is not based on anything that could link the old and new together. This is critical — no names of relatives, no keeping the middle name, etc. It also means that there can no longer be any direct contact between you and relatives or friends back home. All contact should be via an intermediate mail drop or the Internet. We will go into more on how the Internet can be used to enhance a new identity in a later chapter.

As a new-identity seeker, you need to make a list of all the locations where you have relatives and friends, and places you told people you would want to visit or live. These places need to be avoided at all cost. Another excellent strategy is to leave false clues about places where you have no intention of going. One way to do this is to get plane schedules or brochures about certain cities. Just don't overdo it and be too obvious — the cops might spot a set-up.

Once you have gotten to your new locale, you must avoid ever being fingerprinted, especially if the police already have your prints on file. If you are arrested and fingerprinted, your new identity will be exposed quickly. This means giving up whatever criminal activity got you into this predicament. The good news is that if you become a law-abiding citizen and follow carefully the guidelines in creating your identity, you will become one of the small percentage of fugitives wanted for serious crimes who are never caught. There are two reasons for this: First, it takes about six months for a case to cool off and the more recent cases occupy officers' attention. Also, because you are no longer committing crimes, no new information is coming in. The resource limitations of police agencies means assets are assigned where there is the greatest chance of result. When you are no longer dangerous, the impetus to catch you declines.

CHAPTER THREE

The Social Security Number and New Identities

Most identity changers want desperately to get a new, valid Social Security number. A new, valid Social Security number can make many aspects of life easier. The individual can work under the new identity with no problem, establish credit, and even collect Social Security benefits at a later date. In theory, anyone with the necessary documents should have no trouble receiving a new Social Security number. The reality is far different.

The Social Security number (SSN) is the de facto national identity card in America. With just this number and nothing else, numerous records about anyone can be quickly accessed. Most of this use of the Social Security number as a universal identifier happened outside the formal jurisdiction of the law. Consider the use that banks and credit bureaus make of the number. Credit bureaus use the number as a file identification tool. The credit bureau computers segregate individual files from each other via the Social Security number. Banks use account approval services, such as TeleCheck and ChexSystems, to verify that an applicant doesn't have a history of bounced checks. These systems use the name and Social Security number as file identifiers.

Many states use the Social Security number as the driver's license number. This is a grey area of the law. No laws specifically authorize this, but federal law does not prohibit it, either. Health, auto, and life insurance companies frequently require and use the Social Security number as a file identifier. State boards of worker's compensation frequently use the number as a file identifier, and many state licensing agencies use it for such items as business licenses, professional credentials, etc.

The federal government uses the Social Security number as the employee identification number for all federal employees, and the military makes the service number of the individual the Social Security number. When an individual files for bankruptcy in the federal courts, the Social Security number is used as an identifier on the bankruptcy petition.

The Social Security Administration is well aware of the power their assigned number has over the lives of most Americans. As a result, they have made it very difficult for an adult to get a new number unless they fall into one of a small number of categories. The Social Security Administration has also initiated procedures to discourage most new-identity seekers from even considering applying for a new number. Nevertheless, there are ways around these procedures.

Obtaining a New Social Security Number

In Appendix 1 is a reproduction of the application materials for a Social Security number. Some things need to be noticed. First, all applicants eighteen years of age and over must apply in person at the Social Security office. It is mandatory that an interview be conducted with the applicant. Another change is that if the applicant is under eighteen years of age, the Social Security numbers of the parents must be provided. This can be circumvented if the parents are illegal immigrants or visiting foreigners who do not have Social Security numbers. But once again, these are land mines designed to trip up the unprepared.

The applicant for a Social Security card will normally be required to present their birth certificate and a piece of photo identification. These are scanned into the computer along with the application form. If everything is in order, the application is signed off then and there, and no further verification takes place. In three weeks the applicant is mailed a new card from Social Security headquarters outside of Washington, D.C.

If there are doubts about the authenticity of the documents, the Social Security Administration can request verification of the birth certificate and driver's license with the issuing authorities. This will take a few weeks. However, in some cases, if the birth certificate is found to be false, the state that issued the driver's license will be notified and the license will be cancelled.

So how can a person obtain a new Social Security number? The Social Security Administration will assign you a new number if you can show that you have been the victim of identity theft. Nearly one million Americans will be victimized by this crime in 2002, and the Social Security people will be forced to address this issue. This is especially good news for people who use the legal method of identity change.

Establishing Evidence of Identity Theft

Assume that you have changed your identity by the legal method and want a new Social Security number. The first step you must take is to make it appear as if you have been the victim of identity theft. This stage of the plan should be carried out under your current name, not the new name you have received under a name-change order. The Social Security Administration becomes suspicious if you attempt to get a new number with a new name at the same time. This will involve filing the necessary police reports and doing other paperwork to establish your case.

Before you can create this evidence, however, you need to understand how credit bureau computer systems work. Credit bureau computer systems use the Social Security number of the individual as the primary file retrieval tool. When someone applies for credit, their background is checked against information already in the credit bureau computer system. The files are searched by

Social Security number, and when a match is found between the Social Security number being searched and a file, the file is recalled.

At the same time the file is recalled, the address data on the file is updated to reflect the address used by the applicant. In other words, if the address in the file is 123 Main Street, but the applicant now lists 555 Mockingbird Lane, the Mockingbird Lane address will now be listed as the current address, and 123 Main Street will now be listed as a previous address.

Identity thieves have long exploited this aspect of credit bureau computer systems. Once the address has been altered, which happens the first time it is inputted, new credit applications can be made with this new address and it will arouse no suspicion with the creditor. Identity thieves can have new credit cards sent to this address and the victim never knows about it. One indication of identity theft is the listing of addresses on the victim's credit report that he knows nothing about.

You can exploit this feature of the credit bureaus to create evidence of identity theft. Simply fill out a few credit card applications listing an address in another city. These are best done online at a credit card web site that offers instant credit decisions. Your credit report will be pulled immediately and the new address will go right into the system. Do this from a public Internet café, not from your home computer. A couple of weeks later, request a copy of your credit report, and these spurious addresses will appear. Now call the credit card companies where you applied, tell them the credit application was fraudulent, and file a complaint. Make a copy of this. Also file a complaint with your local police department, and with the Federal Trade Commission. A sample of the Federal Trade Commission's identity theft complaint form is reproduced in Appendix 1.

Once you have this legal paperwork, go to the Social Security Administration office. From your paperwork they will attempt to establish two criteria: first, that someone has misused your Social Security number, and; secondly, that you have suffered some harm from this. This harm could be denial of credit or employment, the inability to open a bank account, etc. After this has been established, they will issue you a new number. In a few weeks you will receive a new card in the mail. Once you have received the new card, then go to the Social Security office and apply to get your new name on the card with the new number. This is routine if you have your court name-change order. *Violá!* You now have a new Social Security number in your new name.

Juvenile Application Method

Another method of obtaining a new Social Security number is to use the juvenile application method. You apply claiming to be a teenager, but with the same name as yours. This works, because when employers send in Social Security contributions, they go in only by name and number. The Social Security card itself doesn't have any indication of age on it. To further make this issue congruent, you make the month and date of birth of your teenage self to be the same as yours, with only the year being different. You may not be able to start collecting Social Security benefits when you turn sixty-five, but this is not an important consideration for new identity seekers.

Juvenile applications can be done by mail. The only stumbling block is to have the Social Security number of at least one parent; the mail-in application will arouse no suspicion if you have this. You could make yourself the parent, and create a son or daughter with the name you wish to assume. The other parent could be a foreign national. To do this you will need a high-quality, forged birth certificate. Details on how to forge a birth certificate are provided in other books listed in the Recommended Reading at the end of this book.

A New Identity via Identity Theft

Identity theft is the fastest growing crime in America. Nearly one million people will be victimized by this crime in 2002, and the numbers are growing by nearly fifty percent every year. What exactly is identity theft? In short, identity theft occurs when someone else appropriates your personal identifiers — name, birthdate, driver's license, and credit history, and then passes himself off as you. Most identity thieves are seeking only short-term financial gain. The common practice of identity thieves is to obtain new credit cards and loans in the name of the victim, max them out, and then skip town before the victim ever knows what happened. Complete information on this aspect of identity theft, who is doing it, and steps you can take to protect yourself are given in *Identity Theft: The Cybercrime of the Millennium*, by John Q. Newman.

A natural question would be: Is it possible for an identity thief to steal another person's identity, then live under that identity long-term, and not face detection? In effect, to create a new identity via identity theft? The answer is yes, provided the identity thief is very careful. Certain precautions must be taken, but in some ways, this can even be a preferred method of identity changing.

The advantages to new-identity creation via this method are clear. The person being "created" is real. As a result, all of the foundation documentation is legitimate. The birth certificate is real — no need to create forgeries here. The individual has a real Social Security number, which can make numerous activities easier. The disadvantage to this method is that the real person is also out there in the world and care must be taken to avoid crossing their path — both physically and electronically.

Choosing a Target

The key to making an identity change via identity theft work is carefully choosing the person you intend to become, doing complete background research on that person, and then being very careful in the steps you take in the future. Let us consider the type of person that can be successfully "cloned."

This individual needs to be a pillar-of-the-community type — no criminal record, and not high-profile. He needs to be one of the faceless millions who goes to work every day, pays his bills on time, and is not the subject of court litigation. This person should never be on the evening news. This individual should live far away from where you do, and certainly be out of state. He should also not live anywhere near where you intend to live in the future.

How can you find a person like this? Your own life experience will probably give you a nucleus of people to consider as potential prospects. Former classmates, old buddies, acquaintances from church or other places. You can sit down and make a list. Once you have the names of about five prospects, you will then start confirming what are known as base identifiers — birth dates, full names, addresses, etc. This is very important because it will allow you to make detailed record searches to conclusively determine if any of these people are good prospects.

For each person, you will need to determine if they have a criminal record, have any warrants outstanding, have a good driving record, and where they have lived over the last ten to fifteen years. This last item is very important, because it will let you know which state data systems the target has had files in. For example, if your target has lived in Oregon, Idaho, and Washington State, you know that there is a very good possibility that they will have had driver's licenses and voter registrations in these states. If you later assume this individual's identity, you want to avoid these states.

It is quite easy to check for criminal records on most people. Numerous online record search firms offer these services. You will also need to determine the subject's Social Security number. This is also readily done via one of these firms. Once you have the Social Security number, you can then run a Social Security number trace, which will reveal to you the current and previous addresses of the target. Armed with this information, you then perform criminal-record searches in these locales. In some states, this can be done on a statewide basis because the public has access to the state computer record databases; in other states this must be done by county. Complete information can be found on this subject in *Be Your Own Dick: Private Investigating Made Easy.*

Documenting the New Identity

Once you have determined that the individual is a good target, you can write for a copy of their birth certificate. Once you have this, you can start to document this person in your desired new state of residence. This follows the classic identity-change model — voter registration, library card, etc. Then, you would obtain a state identity card and driver's license. However, some types of identification must be avoided.

You can never get a passport with an identity built via this method. Passports are only issued by the U.S. government, and you would be exposed if the real person later on applied for a passport. Also, you cannot work under the Social Security number assigned to this person. Come tax time, there will be real problems if the IRS has income contributions from two different sources using the same number. There is an alternative to the Social Security number for tax purposes, and this will be discussed in the next section.

The best use of a new identity made this way is as an interim measure until you can create a permanent new identity using the classic methods of identity changing. There is always a small risk that an identity created this way can be discovered.

The Alternative to a Social Security Number

Some new-identity seekers may prefer to completely avoid the Social Security number problem. The use of a number of convenience — a potentially valid, made-up Social Security number — can have problems over the long term, particularly if the user is holding traditional employment. After a while, the employer will receive a notice that the number does not match the employee name, and that they should get it corrected. This usually does not cause much problem, because this happens all the time. Earlier we examined ways in which someone can receive a valid number in any name they want. But what if one wishes to avoid all of this hassle in the first place?

The IRS and Illegal Immigrants

There is now a solution to this problem, provided by the government itself. To understand why and how, we need to look at the massive problem of illegal immigrant workers in the United States.

There are nearly ten million illegal immigrants living right now in America, and six million of these people are in the labor force. One recent study estimated that 25% of all household domestic workers and nearly 10% of all restaurant employees in the United States are illegal immigrants. This was driven home acutely in the aftermath of the World Trade Center attacks, when numerous restaurant and janitorial employees who perished were discovered to have been undocumented workers from Mexico and Central America.

In some parts of the United States, nearly half of the restaurant, janitorial, and domestic employees are illegal immigrants. It is clear that if these people were deported en masse tomorrow, the economics of places such as Southern California and South Texas would cease to function. Employers in these locations commonly look the other way when presented with false documents to establish employment eligibility.

When these illegal immigrants work, they provide their employers with false Social Security numbers. Payroll deductions and Social Security contributions are made under these numbers. Eventually the employer receives notification that the names and numbers do not match. In many instances, the employer simply ignores the notices, as they knew from the outset that the employee was probably not in the country legally.

This widespread use of bogus Social Security numbers creates problems, particularly for the real person whose Social Security number has been appropriated. It has also created problems for the Internal Revenue Service, who gave tax refunds to illegal immigrants. This practice stopped in 1995, when the IRS began verifying the name with the Social Security number on all tax returns. If the name and number do not match, the return is rejected and all deductions are disallowed. However, this created a new set of problems.

The ITIN

The IRS realized that they have no interest in the immigration status of anyone working. Their sole interest is in collecting taxes and not having the tax collection system gummed up with millions of bogus returns. To solve this problem and to face the reality of millions of illegal immigrant workers, the ITIN, or Individual Taxpayer Identification Number, was created. This number is a nine-digit number just like the Social Security number. It can be used by employees on their tax returns, and by an employer remitting payroll taxes. The immigrant can file a tax return and get a refund, but it is not a Social Security number and cannot be used for Social Security benefits. Anyone can get this number, which is issued by the IRS.

On the next few pages we have reproduced the application material for this number. Although this number is technically only for those who cannot get a Social Security number, it is useful for privacy hounds who do not want their Social Security number used by an employer. The ITIN is ideal if you are an identity changer who will start your own business, work as a contract employee, or receive royalty income. This number allows you to receive taxable earnings without any trouble. Many banks will now also accept the ITIN in lieu of a Social Security number when opening up an account. If you work as a contract employee, you simply give this number to the firm paying you. If you own a business and make yourself an employee, you use this number on the earnings you pay yourself. This number also comes in handy for all those nongovernmental forms that ask for a Social Security number. Most places will not realize the difference.

Form **W-7** (Rev. October 1999) Department of the Treasury Internal Revenue Service	**Application for IRS Individual Taxpayer Identification Number** ▶ See instructions. ▶ Please type or print. ▶ For use by individuals who are NOT U.S. citizens, nationals, or permanent residents.	OMB No. 1545-1483

Before you begin:
- *This number is for tax purposes only.* **Do not submit** *this form if you have, or are eligible to obtain, a U.S. social security number (SSN).*
- *Receipt of an IRS individual taxpayer identification number (ITIN) creates no inference regarding your immigration status or your right to work in the United States.*
- *Receipt of an ITIN does not make you eligible to claim the earned income credit (EIC).*

FOR IRS USE ONLY

Reason you are submitting Form W-7. (Check only one box. See instructions.)
- a ☐ Nonresident alien required to obtain ITIN to claim tax treaty benefit
- b ☐ Nonresident alien filing a U.S. tax return and not eligible for an SSN
- c ☐ U.S. resident alien (based on days present in the United States) filing a U.S. tax return and not eligible for an SSN
- d ☐ Dependent of U.S. person ⎱ Enter name and SSN of U.S. person (see instructions) ▶ ....
- e ☐ Spouse of U.S. person ⎰ ....
- f ☐ Other (specify)

1	**Name** (see instructions) Name at birth if different . . ▶	**1a** Last name (surname or family name)	First name	Middle name
		1b Last name (surname or family name)	First name	Middle name

2	**Permanent residence address, if any** (see instructions)	Street address, apartment number, or rural route number. **Do not use a P.O. box number.**
		City or town, state or province, and country. Include ZIP code or postal code where appropriate

3	**Mailing address** (if different from above)	Street address, apartment number, P.O. box number, or rural route number.
		City or town, state or province, and country. Include ZIP code or postal code where appropriate

4	**Birth information**	Date of birth (month, day, year) / /	Country of birth	City and state or province (optional)	5 ☐ Male ☐ Female

6	**Family information**	Father's last name (surname)	First name	Middle name
		Mother's maiden name (surname)	First name	Middle name

7	**Other information**	**7a** Country(ies) of citizenship	**7b** Foreign tax identification number	**7c** Type of U.S. visa (if any) and expiration date

7d Identification document(s) submitted (see instructions).
☐ Passport ☐ Driver's license/State I.D. ☐ INS documentation ☐ Other.....................
Issued by: Number:

7e Have you previously received a U.S. temporary Taxpayer Identification Number (TIN) or Employer Identification Number (EIN)?
☐ No/Do not know. Skip line 7f.
☐ Yes. Complete line 7f. If you need more space, list on a sheet and attach to this form. (See instructions.)

7f TIN ☐☐☐-☐☐-☐☐☐☐   EIN ☐☐-☐☐☐☐☐☐☐
Enter the name under which the TIN was issued | Enter the name under which the EIN was issued

Sign Here
Keep a copy of this form for your records.

Under penalties of perjury, I (applicant/delegate/acceptance agent) declare that I have examined this application, including accompanying documentation and statements, and to the best of my knowledge and belief, it is true, correct, and complete. I authorize the IRS to disclose to my acceptance agent returns or return information necessary to resolve matters regarding the assignment of my IRS individual taxpayer identification number (ITIN)

▶ Signature of applicant (if delegate, see instructions) | Date (month, day, year) / / | Phone number

▶ Name of delegate, if applicable (type or print) | Delegate's relationship to applicant ▶ | ☐ Parent ☐ Guardian ☐ Power of Attorney

Acceptance Agent's Use ONLY
▶ Signature | Date (month, day, year) / / | Phone ( ) Fax ( )
▶ Name and title (type or print) | Name of company | EIN

For Paperwork Reduction Act Notice, see page 4.   Cat. No. 10229L   Form **W-7** (Rev. 10-99)

Form W-7 (Rev. 10-99)

General Instructions

Note: *If you have been lawfully admitted for permanent residence or U.S. employment, you are eligible for a social security number. Do not complete this form.*

Purpose of Form

Use Form W-7 to apply for an IRS individual taxpayer identification number (ITIN). An ITIN is a nine-digit number issued by the U.S. Internal Revenue Service (IRS) to individuals who are required to have a U.S. taxpayer identification number but who do not have, and are not eligible to obtain, a social security number (SSN).

The ITIN is for tax purposes only. It does not entitle you to social security benefits, and creates no inference regarding your immigration status or your right to work in the United States. Any individual who is eligible to be legally employed in the United States must have an SSN.

Note: *Individuals filing tax returns using an ITIN are not eligible for the earned income credit (EIC).*

Who Must Apply

Any individual who is **not eligible to obtain an SSN** but who must furnish a taxpayer identification number to the IRS must apply for an ITIN on Form W-7. For example:

● A nonresident alien individual not eligible for an SSN who is required to file a U.S. tax return OR who is filing a U.S. tax return only to claim a refund.

● A nonresident alien individual not eligible for an SSN who elects to file a joint U.S. tax return with a spouse who is a U.S. citizen or resident.

● A U.S. resident alien (based on substantial presence) who files a U.S. tax return but who is not eligible for an SSN.

● An alien spouse claimed as an exemption on a U.S. tax return who is not eligible to obtain an SSN.

● An alien individual eligible to be claimed as a dependent on a U.S. tax return but who is unable or not eligible to obtain an SSN. To determine if an alien individual is eligible to be claimed as a dependent on a U.S. tax return, see **Pub. 501**, Exemptions, Standard Deduction, and Filing Information, and **Pub. 519**, U.S. Tax Guide for Aliens.

DO NOT complete Form W-7 if you have an SSN **or** you are eligible to obtain an SSN. Thus, do not complete this form if you are a U.S. citizen or national, or if you have been lawfully admitted for permanent residence or U.S. employment.

To obtain an SSN, get **Form SS-5**, Application for a Social Security Card. To get Form SS-5 or to find out if you are eligible to obtain an SSN, contact a Social Security Administration office.

If you have an application for an SSN pending, **do not** file Form W-7. Complete Form W-7 only if the Social Security Administration notifies you that an SSN cannot be issued.

Additional Information

Publications. For details on resident and nonresident alien status and the tests for residence (including the substantial presence test), get Pub. 519.

For details on individuals who can be claimed as dependents and on obtaining an SSN for a dependent, get Pub. 501.

For details on eligibility for the earned income credit, get **Pub. 596**, Earned Income Credit.

These publications are available free from the IRS. To order the publications, call 1-800-TAX-FORM (1-800-829-3676) if you are in the United States. If you have a foreign address, you can write to:

Eastern Area Distribution Center
P.O. Box 85074
Richmond, VA 23261-5074

You can also get these publications using a computer and modem. On the Internet, you can do this in two ways:

World Wide Web: Connect to www.irs.gov.

File transfer protocol: Connect to ftp.irs.gov.

Telephone help. If, after reading these instructions and our free publications, you are not sure how to complete your application or have additional questions, you may call for assistance.

● Inside the United States: 1-800-829-1040. This service is available 24 hours a day, 7 days a week from January 3, 2000, through April 17, 2000. Beginning April 18, 2000, this service is available Monday through Saturday from 7:00 a.m. until 11:00 p.m. local time. Holiday hours may vary.

● Outside the United States: 1-215-516-ITIN (215-516-4846). This is not a toll-free number. You may also contact any of our overseas offices in Berlin, London, Mexico City, Paris, Rome, Singapore, or Tokyo.

How To Apply

You can apply either by mail or in person. See **Where To Apply** on this page. Keep a copy for your records. Be sure to mail or bring with you:

● Your completed Form W-7, and

● The original documents, or certified or notarized copies of documents, that substantiate the information provided on the Form W-7.

The document(s) you present must be current and must verify: **(a)** your identity, that is, contain your name and a photograph, and **(b)** support your claim of foreign status. You may have to provide a combination of documents for this purpose. Examples of acceptable documents include, but are not limited to:

● A passport.

● A driver's license.

● Documents issued by the U.S. Immigration and Naturalization Service (INS).

● An identity card issued by a state or national government authority.

● A foreign military or military dependent identification card.

● A foreign voter registration certificate.

● Birth, marriage, or baptismal certificates.

● School records.

You can submit copies of original documents. However, such documents must be:

● Certified by the issuing agency or official custodian of the original record; or

● Notarized by a U.S. notary public legally authorized within his or her local jurisdiction to certify that the document is a true copy of the original. To do this, the notary must see the valid, unaltered original document and verify that the copy conforms to the original. U.S. notaries public are available at U.S. embassies and consulates worldwide. Non-U.S. notarizations will **not** be accepted.

When To Apply

Complete Form W-7 as soon as you meet one of the requirements listed under **Who Must Apply** on this page. Applying early will give the IRS time to issue you an ITIN before its required use.

If you have not heard from the IRS regarding your ITIN within 30 days, you may call 1-800-829-1040 (in the United States) or 1-215-516-4846 (outside the United States) to find out about the status of your application. Be sure to have a copy of your application available when you call. Please allow 30 days from the date you submitted Form W-7 before calling the IRS about the status of your application.

Allow 4 to 6 weeks for the IRS to notify you in writing of your ITIN.

Where To Apply

Applying in person. You can apply for an ITIN at any IRS walk-in office in the United States and at most IRS offices abroad (contact the IRS office abroad to find out if that office accepts Form W-7 applications). You can also get application forms at certain U.S. consular offices.

You can also apply through an acceptance agent authorized by the IRS.

Applying by mail. Complete Form W-7, sign and date it, and mail the form along with the original or certified or notarized copies of your documentation to:

Internal Revenue Service
Philadelphia Service Center
ITIN Unit
P.O. Box 447
Bensalem, PA 19020

Original documents you submit will be returned to you. You do not need to provide a return envelope. **Copies** of documents will not be returned.

Specific Instructions

The following instructions are for those items that are not self-explanatory. Enter N/A (not applicable) on all lines that do not apply. If you are completing this form for someone else, answer the questions as they apply to that person.

Reason for applying. You must check a box to indicate the reason you are completing this Form W-7. **Check only one box.**

Form W-7 (Rev. 10-99)

a. Nonresident alien required to obtain ITIN to claim tax treaty benefit. Certain nonresident aliens must obtain an ITIN to claim a tax treaty benefit even if they do not have to file a U.S. tax return.

b. Nonresident alien filing a U.S. tax return and not eligible for an SSN. This category includes:

● A nonresident alien who must file a U.S. tax return to report income effectively or not effectively connected with the conduct of a trade or business in the United States.

● A nonresident alien who is filing a U.S. tax return only to obtain a refund.

● A nonresident alien electing to file a U.S. tax return jointly with a spouse who is a U.S. citizen or resident.

c. U.S. resident alien (based on days present in the United States) filing a U.S. tax return and not eligible for an SSN. A foreign individual living in the United States who does not have permission to work from the INS, and is thus ineligible for an SSN, may still have a U.S. tax return filing obligation. Such individuals must check this box.

d. Dependent of U.S. person. This is an individual who may be claimed as a dependent on a U.S. tax return and who is unable, or not eligible, to obtain an SSN.

Note: *A U.S. person is a citizen, national, or resident alien of the United States.*

e. Spouse of U.S. person. This is a nonresident alien husband or wife who is not filing a U.S. tax return (including a joint return) but who may be claimed as a spouse for an exemption, and who is not eligible to obtain an SSN.

f. Other. Use this box **only** if your situation does not fall into any of the above categories. If you check this box, you must describe in detail your reason for requesting an ITIN.

SSN of U.S. person. If you are applying for an ITIN under category **d** or **e** above, you **must** provide the **full name and SSN** of the U.S. person. Enter the information in the space provided. If the U.S. person chooses to provide this information in a separate letter, be sure to enter "Information will be provided in separate letter" in this space. If this space is left blank, your application will be rejected.

The letter provided by the U.S. person must identify the Form W-7 to which the information relates and must include:

● The U.S. person's full name and SSN; **and**

● The name, address, date of birth and country of birth of the dependent or spouse as shown on the Form W-7.

Mail the letter to the address shown under **Where To Apply** on page 3.

Note: *If the U.S. person chooses this method, the Form W-7 will not be processed until the information is received.*

Lines 1a and 1b. Enter your legal name on line 1a. This entry should reflect your name as it will appear on your U.S. tax return. If your legal name was different at birth, enter on line 1b your name at birth as it appears on your birth certificate.

Line 2. Enter your complete address in the country where you permanently or normally reside. If you are claiming a benefit under an income tax treaty with the United States, the address entered must normally be an address in the treaty country. Include the postal code where appropriate.

Do not use a Post Office box or an "in care of" (c/o) address instead of a street address. It will not be accepted.

Line 3. Enter your mailing address if it is different from the address on line 2. This is the address the IRS will use to mail you written notification of your ITIN.

Line 4. You **must** identify the country in which you were born.

Line 7b. If your country of residence for tax purposes has issued you a tax identification number, enter that number on line 7b. For example, if you are a resident of Canada, you would enter your Canadian Social Insurance Number.

Line 7c. Enter only U.S. nonimmigrant visa information, for example, "B-1/B-2." Also enter the expiration date of the visa.

Line 7d. If you have a passport, use it to provide verification of your identity and foreign status. Check the "Passport" box.

If you do not have a passport, use a driver's license or official identification card issued by a U.S. or foreign governmental jurisdiction and check the appropriate box.

If you are using documents issued by the INS, check the "INS documentation" box.

If you have none of the above, check the box for "Other" and **specifically identify** the type(s) of document you are using (for example, enter "military ID" for a military or military/dependent identification card). You may have to provide more than one current document to verify your identity and foreign status. At least one document you present should contain a recent photograph.

You must provide the name of the state, country, or other issuer, and the identification number (if any) appearing on the document(s) you provide. You may be required to provide a translation of documents in a foreign language.

Line 7e. If you ever received a "temporary Taxpayer Identification Number" (TIN) or an Employer Identification Number (EIN), check the "Yes" box and enter the number on line 7f. If you never had a temporary TIN or an EIN, or you do not know your temporary TIN, check the "No/Do not know" box.

A "temporary TIN" was a nine-digit number issued by the IRS to individuals before 1996. You would have been issued this number if you filed a U.S. tax return and did not have a social security number. This temporary TIN will appear on any correspondence the IRS sent you concerning that return. You may have been issued more than one temporary TIN. If so, attach a separate sheet listing all the temporary TINs you received.

An EIN is a nine-digit number assigned by the IRS to businesses, such as sole proprietorships.

Line 7f. Enter in the space provided the temporary TIN and/or EIN and the name under which the number was issued.

Signature. Generally, Form W-7 **must be signed by the applicant.** However, if the applicant is a minor 14 years of age or younger, a delegate (parent or guardian) should sign for him or her. Type or print the delegate's name in the space provided and check the appropriate box to indicate the relationship to the applicant.

If the applicant is over 14 years of age, the applicant may appoint an authorized agent to sign. The authorized agent must print his or her name in the space provided for the name of the delegate and must attach **Form 2848,** Power of Attorney and Declaration of Representative.

Paperwork Reduction Act Notice. We ask for the information on this form to carry out the Internal Revenue laws of the United States. You are required to give us the information. We need it to ensure that you are complying with these laws and to allow us to figure and collect the right amount of tax.

You are not required to provide the information requested on a form that is subject to the Paperwork Reduction Act unless the form displays a valid OMB control number. Books or records relating to a form or its instructions must be retained as long as their contents may become material in the administration of any Internal Revenue law. Generally, tax returns and return information are confidential, as required by Internal Revenue Code section 6103.

The time needed to complete and file this form will vary depending on individual circumstances. The estimated average time is: **Learning about the law or the form,** 13 min.; **Preparing the form,** 29 min.; **Copying, assembling, and sending the form to the IRS,** 20 min.

If you have comments concerning the accuracy of these time estimates or suggestions for making this form simpler, we would be happy to hear from you. You can write to the Tax Forms Committee, Western Area Distribution Center, Rancho Cordova, CA 95743-0001. **DO NOT** send the form to this address. Instead, see **Where To Apply** on page 3.

CHAPTER FOUR

The Delayed Birth Certificate

A new wrinkle on new identity creation involves obtaining a real, valid birth certificate. This involves having the state issue you a delayed certificate of birth registration. Once this has been done, you can then proceed to use this document to obtain other real identification. The advantage of this method is that it nets you a genuine birth certificate that can later be verified. How does one go about getting a delayed birth certificate, and are there any drawbacks to using this method of identity creation?

Universal birth registration is a practice that is relatively recent. Although most states have had laws on the books requiring universal birth registration for a century or longer, the reality was frequently different. In many Southern states, the birth of rural blacks was routinely not registered, and many births were not registered for one reason or another even in Northern states. Reasons for this could have been a child born out of wedlock, a child born of rape, or a child of a different race born to a white female. As a result, although it is not a common thing to meet people with no birth certificate, it is not an exceedingly rare occurrence either.

The Vital Statistics Search

Because of these facts, all states have a procedure whereby they can issue a delayed birth certificate to someone whose birth was not properly registered. This procedure always begins with a search of the vital statistics records. Typically the person will have some notion of what his birthdate and birthplace is. The individual writes to the state vital statistics bureau requesting a search of the records for his birth certificate. When no record is found, the vital statistics people will usually search a year before and after the birthdate for the record. When there is still no record found, the vital statistics bureau will then send a letter to the applicant certifying that a search of the records was made and no certificate was found. This statement begins the process by which someone can obtain a delayed birth certificate.

States vary as to the complexity of the process to create a delayed birth certificate. In general, the procedure involves the applicant submitting secondary evidence of their birth and age. This can include such items as school records, notarized affidavits from people who know the applicant, church or religious records, insurance policies, membership records, etc. Once all of the evidence has been received, it is reviewed. If the applicant has met the burden of proof, a new birth certificate will be issued.

Choosing a State of Birth

The strategy with this approach is to pick a state that makes the burden as small as possible. The second part of the strategy involves submitting documents that are difficult if not impossible to verify. At the end of the chapter is a reproduction of information from the state of Iowa on the delayed birth certificate procedure in that state. Someone considering this route should write away to a number of states before deciding on which one to choose.

If the applicant is successful, he will net himself a birth certificate. But this will not be a normal birth certificate. It will prominently say "delayed" certificate of birth across its face. Some federal agencies, particularly the passport office, may not be willing to accept this document until it is a few years old. Because it looks different, it clearly draws attention to itself. An individual using a birth record such as this should clearly have a good cover story prepared as to why his birth was not registered. Aside from this, it seems that the potential benefits outweigh any drawbacks with this method, provided careful attention is paid to details. For instance, use high-quality forgeries when applying for the delayed birth certificate, and be ready to answer any questions that might be posed to you by the vital statistics bureau. As usual, it is always best to create your new birth record in a faraway state, certainly not the one you are living in. This will avoid the possibility of your being asked to come down to the office in person.

State of Iowa

Terry E. Branstad, Governor

DEPARTMENT OF PUBLIC HEALTH
Christopher G. Atchison, Director

Dear Applicant:

When your birth in Iowa has not been previously recorded, you may file a "Delayed Certificate of Birth." Please submit the following items to file a Delayed Certificate of Birth.

(1)   A completed Delayed Certificate of Birth form which has been signed before a notary public by the person whose birth is to be registered. If the individual is under the age of 16 years or is legally incompetent, it must be signed by one of the parents or legal guardian.

(2)   Three documents (or copies of) which, when combined, verify these facts of birth.
   a.   Full name at the time of birth
   b.   Date of birth
   c.   City/town and county of birth
   d.   Mother's full maiden name
   e.   Father's full name

The documents must have been established a minimum of five years prior to the request for Delayed Certificate of Birth for an individual age 7 years or older.

Supporting documents for Delayed Certificate of Birth for a child under the age of 7 years must have been established at least 1 year prior to request.

If the Delayed Certificate of Birth is requested for Social Security or Passport application, documents which were established early in life are more acceptable verification. You should also check with the above two agencies first to see if they will accept a delayed record of birth.

Examples of documents which may verify the facts of birth are attached to this instruction sheet.

The Clerk of District Court in your county can assist you with completing the certificate and can review your documents.

The fee for processing and filing a Delayed Certificate of Birth is $10.00. An additional $10.00 fee is required if you wish to receive a certified copy. All fees are payable by check or money order to the Department of Public Health.

The completed, notarized Delayed Certificate of Birth, supporting documents and fees should be mailed to:

Bureau of Support Services
Vital Records
Iowa Department of Public Health
Lucas State Office Building
Des Moines, Iowa 50319-0075

Your Delayed Certificate of Birth will be processed approximately 15 working days after it is received at the Iowa Department of Public Health. After viewing your documents we may require additional documents. If you have any questions, please call the Delayed Certificate Clerk at (515) 281-5872.

Examples of Supporting Documents

Birth certificate of a child.

Religious record: Baptismal or confirmation records generally list full birth name and dates of birth.

Family Biblic records.

Military entry or discharge papers.

Marriage Certificate: State or County certificate copy generally show age, birthplace, and name of parents.

Employment record.

School record: Available from the Area Education Association. You may contact your local school system to obtain the location of the Area Education Association Office for the school district you attended.

Social Security Application: A copy of your original Social Security Application may be obtained by writing to:

Department of Health, Education and Welfare
Social Security Administration
Baltimore, Maryland 21235
1-800-772-1213

Life Insurance Policy or Pension Plan: You may submit a statement prepared by the company which reflects birthdate and effective date of insurance policy or enrollment in retirement plan.

Hospital or Physician Record: Copy of hospital/physician record which provides facts of birth or a statement reflecting the facts of birth which includes the date of original record.

Cert. No._____

IOWA DEPARTMENT OF PUBLIC HEALTH
VITAL RECORDS SECTION

Delayed Certificate of Birth

Full name
at birth _____
First   Middle   Last

Date of
birth _____ Race _____ Sex _____
(Month)   (Day)   (Year)

Birthplace_____ Iowa _____
(City or Town)

Father: Full
Name _____ Birth-
place _____
(State or Country)

Mother: Maiden
Name _____ Birth-
place _____
(State or Country)

Affidavit: I hereby declare upon oath that the above statements are true.

Signature: _____ Address _____
(To be signed by registrant if possible)

Subscribed and sworn to me on _____ 19 _____

My commission expires on _____ 19 _____

(SEAL)
_____
Notary Public

FOR STATE OFFICE USE ONLY

	ABSTRACT OF SUPPORTING EVIDENCE Name and kind of document and by whom issued and signed	Date original document was made
1		
2		
3		

INFORMATION CONCERNING REGISTRANT AS STATED IN DOCUMENTS

	Birth date or age	Birthplace	Name of Father	Maiden Name of Mother
1				
2				
3				

Additional information: _____

_____
Statement of Reviewing Official

I hereby certify that no prior certificate has been found in the County or State Registrar's Office for this registrant and that documentary evidence has been seen and read which substantiates the facts as set forth in the foregoing abstract.

Signature _____
Chief Bureau of Vital Records/Statistics

CFN-588-0040 (2/88)
CPA-27493

Date
Filed _____

USE <u>BLACK</u> INK OR TYPEWRITER RIBBON

CHAPTER FIVE

New Identity and the AIDS Age

"Wanted: one white male, 30 to 45, dying of AIDS or some other incurable disease, for financial partnership. Call 555-7768."

An advertisement like this might appear in a newspaper classified section in the near future. It is one of the latest methods of identity changing, made possible by the AIDS epidemic. Tens of thousands of people are dying the slow, agonizing death of the late stages of HIV infection. These individuals are typically destitute — having exhausted all of their insurance benefits — and no longer able to work. These hapless individuals form one side of this new identity equation.

On the other side of the equation are healthy persons — usually heterosexual, white males — who want a second chance at life. These men want to leave behind a troubled past that might include bankruptcy, divorce, or even civil and criminal legal problems. The traditional methods of identity changing do not interest these people because of the risk and enormous amount of work necessary to fabricate a new identity out of thin air. Nor do they want to use the classic "dead infant" method of procuring a new birth certificate. These methods also bring with them the risk of exposure. A forty-year-old man applying for his first Social Security card or driver's license will face a lot of scrutiny by identification-issuing bureaucrats. One slipup and the new-identity seeker could be on his way to jail.

Benefits and Advantages

When two sides of this equation connect, a mutually beneficial outcome for each can result. The seeker of the new identity can offer the terminally ill person financial security during those last days. A few hundred dollars a month will provide the opportunity to remain in one's home, eat decent food, and live out the last days with dignity.

The seeker of a new identity obtains an identity that has already been documented with a real Social Security number, driver's license, and other documents. After the real owner dies, or even before, the new-identity seeker can step into this ready-made identity with a minimum of fuss.

What are the advantages of obtaining a new identity this way? The odds are very good that, with the exception of the medical problem, the acquired identity has no serious negative records or other drawbacks, such as outstanding arrest warrants or criminal records. Any financial black marks, such as late bill payments, were probably due to the illness. The acquirer of the new identity can bring these bills up to date and be on his way to a solid credit history in a short period of time. The question in many minds is, in this age of computerized databanks, what specific steps must be done to successfully pull off this type of identity borrowing or transferring?

Covering Your Bases

The first step involves making sure that the future decedent does not die in the same county or state where he was born. This is critical, because most county registrars cross index birth and death records of those who die in the same county of birth. A few states do the same on a statewide basis. California is an example of this.

It is essential to avoid such cross-indexing so that the birth certificate will stay clean in the future. If the individual "taking over" for John Smith needs a copy of "his" birth certificate in three years, it will still be available without any problems.

The next step involves the Social Security Administration. When a person dies, if the relatives of the deceased apply for the Social Security Death Benefit, the Social Security number of the deceased is retired and placed into a database known as the Social Security Death Index, SSDI. This database is updated quarterly and is widely used by credit bureaus and other government agencies to detect people using the Social Security numbers of dead people.

The key thing to remember is that the Social Security number does not get into the database just because the person dies. It gets into the database because the death benefit is claimed. The payment of a death benefit is official confirmation in the eyes of the Social Security Administration that the individual has, in fact, died. If the death benefit is not claimed — it is only $300 — the number will not get into this file.

Identity Documents

The next items that must be handled carefully are the other identification documents of the deceased. The motor vehicle department, passport, and other agencies should not be notified of the death. When these agencies are notified of a death, they cancel all identity documents issued to that person and list the person as deceased in their computer records. This effectively prevents this identity from being used by another person in the future.

Another strategy is to obtain a new license before the terminally ill person has died. This is easier to do than it seems. It is necessary that the individual whose identity is to be acquired bear a general resemblance to the acquirer. The same race, eye and hair color, and height and weight are necessary. One can proceed by either of two methods.

The acquirer can go to a motor vehicle department office in the same state and claim that he has lost his license. If he has supporting documentation, such as birth certificate and Social Security card, the clerk may well issue a duplicate license on the spot.

The only danger is if the clerk can call up an electronic image of the real license holder. If the imposter looks very different and the photo on file is not very old, you might have some difficult explaining to do.

A simpler method involves going to a nearby state with the birth certificate and Social Security card, and applying for an identity card in that state. When the clerk asks if the imposter already holds a driver's license, he would answer yes, and tell him from which state, but state that it is lost. The clerk can verify the out-of-state license on the computer. This ruse can often net a new license in a new state.

Once the decedent's old documents have been replaced with new ones bearing the acquirer's likeness, he can safely start to make plans for living under the name of the deceased. However, some precautions must be taken.

The new life needs to start hundreds — if not thousands — of miles away from where the real individual died. Some records of the death will exist. A death certificate will be filed with the county and a funeral notice might be posted in the newspaper. The family of the deceased will probably not know about the arrangement between the dearly departed and the imposter. If they did, they would likely go to the police.

Another way the imposter permanently separates himself from the deceased is to change the deceased's name in a faraway state. Once the change-of-name is obtained, he can then get a new driver's license and other identification issued in this name. He can also obtain a new Social Security number. We explained in a previous chapter how to make it appear as if you have been the victim of identity theft. This same procedure could be used in this case to obtain a new Social Security number for the deceased.

CHAPTER SIX

Fake ID and Its Role in New-Identity Creation

The terms fake ID, new identity, and fraudulent identification are often used interchangeably. They are not the same, however, and we need to define them for purposes of discussion. Fake identification is any identity document or certificate that purports itself to be a real, validly issued instrument when, in fact, it is not. Fake identification would encompass all manner of forged documents, regardless of their quality. An excellent forgery of a driver's license or passport is still a forgery. A fake college transcript, no matter how masterfully done, is still bogus.

A new identity is a created identity that has been documented with real papers, duly issued by the respective governmental and private organizations. When done correctly, a new identity is indistinguishable from a real person. This new identity has all of the data in the system that a real person does and over time, as this identity becomes seasoned, only a very expensive investigation could prove it to be a construct.

Fraudulent identification is any real identification that is obtained from government and private agencies under a pretext. Thus, a new identity is documented with fraudulent identification, which is 100% valid. The chief goal of a new-identity seeker is to document the new identity with valid, fraudulently issued papers. A fraudulently issued driver's license can safely be used to drive with, because if police stop the holder, the license will pass the police computer check.

Fake ID as an Interim Measure

When an individual is in the early stages of creating a new identity, there may be times when it is necessary to use fake identification as an interim to documenting the assumed identity with real identification. It is necessary to know what are safe and unsafe uses of such fake identification.

Foundation Documents

The most common uses of fake identification are for so-called foundation documents. This would include such items as birth certificates and baptismal records. Forgeries are acceptable for these items, if they are of high-quality. The reason for this is that birth and baptismal certificates themselves are not used as operational identification documents in the United States. These documents are used to establish birth so that one can obtain such items as state identity cards, driver's licenses, passports, etc. A second reason that high-quality forgeries of these documents are acceptable is that they are difficult to verify, and if a forgery is of high enough quality, it will be accepted.

Other certificates can also fit into this category. College transcripts, and award certificates, for instance, can be used in the early stages to help flesh out a new identity. Once a driver's license has been obtained, the fake birth record may never have to be used again. In many instances, a college or high school transcript can be used as proof of identity at a motor vehicle office.

The Fake Driver's License

There are also sellers of fake driver's licenses and state identification cards, as well as fake identification documents. These too, can be used, but only when appropriate, and they should be discarded when no longer needed. Consider a fake driver's license. It should never be used to drive a car, because it will not pass verification with the police unless it is a high-quality duplicate of a valid state license, with the name and license number of an actual license holder on it. It should never be used in any situation where it can be subjected to verification. That having been said, it can be smartly used for many other purposes.

Let us assume an individual is building a new identity and needs to rent an apartment in their new name right away. Instead of waiting for months to get a real license in the new name, they could purchase a high-quality fake license. This license could then be shown to the landlord as proof of identity to get the apartment. A fake license could also be used to purchase airplane or train tickets if it is desired to travel under the assumed name before real documentation can be obtained.

The critical point to remember with fake ID is to always obtain the real equivalent if possible. Fake ID should only be used as a transitional step on your way to valid documents. At some point, all documentation, with the exception of the birth certificate, should be real, government-issued identification. If you use fake ID, always know what the real document looks like, and only use fakes which closely resemble the real item. A second precaution is to use fake ID from a faraway state. This adds another layer of security.

CHAPTER SEVEN

Background Investigations

Most Americans will face some level of scrutiny of their background. This scrutiny of their past may be performed for any number of reasons. It is now very common for employers to perform pre-employment background checks on potential new employees. Many landlords perform similar checks, along with banks and insurance companies. The events of September 11, 2001, make background investigations more common for all levels of employment. No longer are they limited to jobs requiring a security clearance.

The primary motivation for the popularity of the background investigation in America today is financial. Companies can face increased liability if they hire employees who later harm someone. An example of this could be a worker who is hired to drive a company car. If this employee later causes an accident while using a company car, the corporation can be held liable for increased damages if it turns out that the employee had a prior conviction for drunk driving or numerous traffic citations for speeding.

Banks screen anyone wishing to open a checking or savings account, to avoid opening accounts for people who habitually bounce checks or have a history of running up large overdrafts and not paying them off. Landlords want to avoid renting to tenants who will damage expensive apartments or not pay the rent, resulting in the long, expensive process of eviction.

The Negative Record "Underclass"

Most people are not aware how much information employers, banks, landlords, and just about anyone else can access about them, especially in the Internet age and with the vast computerization of many databases. This has created an underclass of people who cannot obtain a decent job or open a bank account, and who even face difficulty finding a place to live.

The one common trait among almost all of these people is that they have "negative" records in databases that are commonly checked during background investigations. For some, a criminal record will preclude employment; for others, a history of bounced checks might force them to use high-priced check-cashing services to manage their finances. In fact, one of the more insidious results of the background-checking craze is that an entire industry has been created that feeds off of those who have been denied access to traditional employment, bank accounts, telephones, etc.

The rapid growth of the check-cashing and payday-loan industry is a good example of this parallel economy. Check-cashing stores proliferate, cashing the payroll and government checks of those whom the banking industry will not allow to have deposit accounts. The payday-loan industry gouges those who can still maintain a checking account, but cannot qualify for traditional loans or credit cards. Similar parallel services exist for telephones and other necessities.

The following pages explain how background investigations are conducted, from a detailed pre-employment investigation run on an applicant for a job requiring a government security clearance, to the quick background check run by a bank before they open a checking account. Some kinds of background checks can be "beaten" and some kinds need to be avoided, particularly by a person living under a new identity. There are certain strategies that can be used to avoid exposure of a new identity by a background check.

The Past Leads to the Present

The first step in learning how to pass background investigations involves understanding how a person generates a paper trail as they move through life, and where these records are located.

Nearly every person who is living, or has lived, has created a set of records that document that life. The first official paperwork most people generate is their birth certificate, and the last, the death certificate. In between these two documents is a literal storehouse of records. It is via this treasure trove of personal data that background investigations accomplish their work.

Many of these records are private, but many are considered to be public records, which means that they can be retrieved by anyone who is interested in seeing them. A short inventory of places where the typical individual has records includes the following:

- ☐ Motor Vehicle Department
- ☐ County Election Board
- ☐ County Assessor's or Recorder's Office
- ☐ Passport Office
- ☐ Civil Court
- ☐ Vital Statistics Bureau
- ☐ Bankruptcy Court
- ☐ University or College Records
- ☐ Internet
- ☐ Law Enforcement Databases

Public Records

This is but a short list of the many places people have records. What is instructive about this list is that most of the records given are considered to be public records. It is the vast and easy availability of public records that allows background investigators to compile a detailed file on most people relatively easily.

Consider your driver's license record. Most people wrongly assume that their record with the motor vehicle department is private. One would certainly think so, judging by the great production most states make of protecting driver privacy when people are in their offices. However, information they guard at the front door, they quite literally shovel out of the back door.

Most states sell their entire driver database, en masse, to anyone who wishes to purchase it. The biggest purchasers of the motor vehicle databases are automobile insurance companies. This is how they learn about your speeding tickets, and raise your rates. It is also how they locate new auto insurance prospects. Driving records are also commonly consulted by employers conducting pre-employment background checks, even if the employee will not be using a company vehicle. Employers know that a driving record that shows a history of speeding tickets or a drunk driving citation will frequently indicate an unreliable employee.

Criminal records can also be accessed, although not in the same way the police do. Police agencies have access to a centralized database maintained by the FBI that contains the criminal conviction data for everyone with a record of a serious misdemeanor or felony offense anywhere in the United States. This database, known as Triple I, is not available to most nongovernmental investigators. However, criminal records are available from county courthouses in all locations. A number of states also allow public access to their statewide database of criminal conviction information. The problem with these records is that some states also release arrest records, even if the charges are dropped before trial or the person is acquitted. Many employers will not hire an individual with an arrest record, even though no conviction resulted.

Worker Compensation Records

A small number of states allow access to their worker's compensation records. This can be a real problem for an individual who was on employment disability for a legitimate reason. Even though it is technically against the law to refuse to hire someone because they have made a worker's compensation claim in the past, many employers do. Many companies consider worker's compensation legalized stealing, and if they find out a job applicant has claimed benefits, they will turn down the application. Of course, a different reason will be given to the applicant. The real reason for the turndown is further masked because often an outside investigation firm will be responsible for actually performing the background investigation. The following states allow open access to worker's compensation files:

Alaska	Arkansas	Connecticut	Illinois	Iowa
Kansas	Maine	Maryland	New Jersey	Oklahoma

In a drive to reduce potential costs, some employers will even check records that have nothing at all to do with employment. For example, an employer may seek to avoid hiring people with risky hobbies, because these individuals might wind up injured and unable to work, or they might make more use of employer-paid health insurance. Employers have been known to check if potential employees have hunting licenses or even pilot credentials as a way to eliminate these risks from their work force.

Certain types of employers have specialized databases. Retail stores check potential employees against databases maintained by companies who keep files on people suspected of stealing from their employers. Retailers justify this practice by noting that 60% of retail theft is committed by employees, not customers.

Credit Reports

The credit report is used to confirm a variety of details about the applicant. In the fine print on most employment applications is a waiver that allows the employer full access to your credit report. This access is requested regardless of the type of job applied for, and even if the employment has nothing to do with handling company money. The use of credit files as a pre-employment screening tool is relatively rare with small companies, but routine with large national corporations.

Credit reports are also widely used by landlords of apartment buildings to screen potential tenants. When people apply to rent an apartment, they typically complete two different forms. The first form is a lease agreement and the second is the formal "application for tenancy," which is really just an authorization to allow the landlord to access your credit report.

Both landlords and employers look for certain items on the credit report. One big item is a bankruptcy filing. Bankruptcy remains on the credit report for ten years, and many landlords automatically reject any tenant who has filed for it. They justify this practice because it takes many months to evict someone for nonpayment of rent. They feel if an individual went completely bankrupt, they might have stuck a past landlord with unpaid rent. Many employers have a similar policy.

The employer and landlord look at the bill-paying history and see if there are a lot of seriously delinquent accounts. The landlord is concerned with the total amount of monthly payments the potential tenant must make. If the total payments are too high, the tenant might be late on the rent because of the excessive commitments elsewhere.

The credit report can also act as a secondary verification of name, birth date, and Social Security number. It can be used to determine if the applicant's background matches what was listed on the job application or tenancy form. Credit reports will show the two previous addresses, and they frequently contain information about the previous employer. Serious discrepancies between what is claimed on the application and what is contained in the credit report can indicate a need for more careful examination of the applicant.

The Key to Passing a Background Check

A background investigation can vary widely, depending on how complete it needs to be, but all background investigations will use some combination of the information sources we have just examined. The key to passing a background investigation is to understand the type of investigation you will face, and then make sure that the information sources consulted will confirm the background you wish to present. This is a most important consideration for a person who is living under a new identity. Many people have had their perfectly documented new identities unmasked during a pre-employment background investigation because they failed to anticipate that they might face a scrutiny of their new name.

The good news is that most background investigations can be passed by people living under a new identity or by those with "bad" records in their past. If you understand the system, you can manipulate it and create positive records where you need them. On the other hand, there are certain types of background investigations that will always turn up a new identity, and must be avoided at all costs.

CHAPTER EIGHT

Passive Investigations

The most common type of background investigation is the passive investigation. The passive background investigation is the type that is performed by most employers and by state and local government agencies. It is also performed by the federal government for employment that does not require a security clearance. Passive investigations are also known as "negative" investigations, because the focus of the investigator is on a lack of negative records in certain databases.

The Searches

A passive investigation starts with what is known as a national agency check. This involves checking for a criminal record, contacting the Internal Revenue Service to confirm that taxes have been paid, and checking to see if the individual is the subject of any current civil litigation. The last two items are normally only checked by federal agencies, or at a private corporation if the employment is very sensitive.

The credit report is pulled and used to confirm the Social Security number, past addresses, and financial status of the applicant. The driving record is examined to make sure that the applicant has not been convicted of drunk driving and does not have excessive speeding tickets.

The passive investigation seeks to verify past educational attainment. Typically, the applicant is allowed to supply proof of degrees and other qualifications. This is usually done through college transcripts and certificates. These are accepted at face value, provided they look authentic and the applicant has not given the interviewer any reason to doubt his qualifications. This is another feature of the passive investigation: a willingness to accept documents at face value if they appear to be genuine.

The same approach is taken when verifying the previous work history. If the applicant has letters of reference from previous employers, they are accepted as long as they appear genuine. If the applicant provides addresses and telephone numbers of supposed previous employers they will be contacted for confirmation. But most importantly, the background checker will accept them as being legitimate. As long as someone answers the inquiry (see Chapter 11), no attempt will be made to determine if the Acme Corporation of Spokane is actually a real company.

Limits of the Passive Investigation

The passive investigation is the most common type of background investigation because it balances the need to check out new applicants with the financial realities of modern business. Corporations cannot afford to spend hundreds of dollars on each applicant to verify the credentials and backgrounds of thousands of workers, and in the same way, small firms cannot afford to spend large sums of money vetting each applicant for a position.

A passive investigation will detect most people who have criminal records or poor backgrounds in general. A passive investigation will not detect a person who is living under a new identity if the person with the new identity has been careful to lay his groundwork in advance. Passive investigations can also be defeated by people under their real identities who have undesirable items in their past, such as poor credit, criminal convictions, or a spotty employment record.

Fingerprinting

How can you know if it is a passive investigation? One giveaway will be if fingerprints are required. Fingerprinting usually indicates that it is not just a passive investigation. There are a few exceptions to this rule, however.

Some states require certain types of workers to be fingerprinted. Many states require all people who work in public school districts to be fingerprinted, and if you work in the casino industry in Nevada, even in a nongambling-related function, such as housekeeping, you will have to be fingerprinted. In both of these situations, the fingerprinting is just part of a passive investigation. In some cases, a person living under a new identity can pass these screenings, but in other cases they must be avoided.

The basic rule is that if you have already been fingerprinted under your old identity, no matter how long ago, you must avoid being fingerprinted under your new identity. If you have never been fingerprinted before, you can safely be fingerprinted as part of a passive investigation. The reason for this needs to be clarified.

Fingerprints are highly prized by law enforcement agencies because they are a virtually perfect way to positively identify an individual. Every state maintains a vast computerized repository of fingerprint files, and there is a national database maintained by the FBI. Anytime a person is arrested or fingerprinted by a government agency or the military, their fingerprints make their way into the federal fingerprint repository and that of the state where the arrest takes place.

The procedure is also followed when fingerprints are voluntarily submitted as part of a background check. The government does not simply look for a fingerprint match, and when none is found, return back a statement attesting to that fact. The fingerprints submitted are now digitized and entered into the computer. Many people living under new identities have failed to understand this to their peril. The FBI takes the attitude that once they have an individual's fingerprints, regardless of the reason, they want to keep them on file.

So if an individual is living under a new identity, but was fingerprinted 25 years ago under their real name, they must avoid any job where the background investigation will require a fingerprint check. If this advice is not followed, the following scenario can happen.

The Sheriff's Card: A Scenario

Suppose a person living under a new identity applies for a janitorial job at a Nevada casino. In the state of Nevada, anyone working in an establishment with a gaming license must have what is known locally as a "sheriff's card" to work. One must have this card even if the worker is employed in a nongambling capacity such as the restaurant service, housekeeping, janitorial, etc. The local sheriff or police department in the municipality of residence issues this card. On the next page we have reproduced the form that must be completed by applicants.

The form allows the police to make three types of computer searches immediately. The first is for any outstanding arrest warrants. This search is made on the wanted persons index, of the NCIC, described in Chapter 2. The second check is made of the local wanted persons index to see if there are any minor offense warrants that are not included on the FBI system. If the applicant has an out-of-state license or identification, a computer check is made at the state's local warrant database to see if a minor warrant is outstanding there. If these checks are passed, the applicant will then be checked for a criminal record. The first criminal record check is on the Interstate Identification Index Database, or Triple I, which is also maintained by the FBI on NCIC. The Triple I check should reveal if the applicant has a conviction for a felony or serious misdemeanor anywhere in the United States.

The police also check the central criminal repository in Nevada and the state repositories in previous states of residence for minor crime convictions that are not reported to Triple I. If these checks are passed, the applicant is photographed, fingerprinted, and issued their sheriff's card.

But the process is not quite over. Notice that on the front of the form, the applicant is asked if they have ever been arrested, not just if they have ever been convicted of a crime. This is very important. Anytime someone is arrested, with few exceptions, they are fingerprinted, which means a fingerprint file will already exist with the FBI repository. Or if our applicant was fingerprinted fifteen years ago for, say, service in the military, his prints are also in the FBI file, under his real name. When the fingerprints taken in Nevada are sent electronically to the FBI, the computer will eventually match the new prints with the ones already on file. Nevada will receive the original information already on file, and now the new name and birth date will be revealed as an alias, and even worse, the police computers will now link the new name and real name together. Needless to say, the sheriff's card will be cancelled and the applicant will face some uncomfortable questions from the local police.

Work Card Application

LAS VEGAS METROPOLITAN POLICE DEPARTMENT
WORK CARD APPLICATION
NON—GAMING (LAS VEGAS)

FINGERPRINT SECTION
601 EAST FREMONT
LAS VEGAS, NEVADA 89101-2985
8AM - 4PM   MON - FRI

READ INSTRUCTIONS ON BACK

DO NOT WRITE IN THIS SPACE	
ID#	
PREV. OR ARREST INFO.	
INTERVIEWING TECH:	
FPC	

☐ ORIGINAL
☐ RENEWAL
☐ CO. LOCATION
☐ CITY LOCATION

Name of Establishment

Address of Establishment

Position

Social Security #

Alias and/or Maiden Name

Name   (first)   (middle)   (last)

Sex	Race	Height	Weight	Hair Color	Eye Color	Age	Date of Birth	Place of Birth

Marks, Scars and Tattoos

US Citizen? ☐ Yes ☐ No
Naturalization #   Passport #   Alien Card #

Local Address   Street & #   Apt. # or Space   City   State   Zip   Phone #

In Case of Emergency Notify: Name *(first, middle, last)*   Relationship   Address *(number, street, city, state, zip)*   Phone #

LIST YOUR CURRENT EMPLOYER BELOW & LIST EACH JOB HELD IN PAST FIVE YEARS. (USE OTHER SIDE OF FORM FOR ADDITIONAL SPACE)

NAME	LOCATION	POSITION	FROM-TO	REASON FOR LEAVING

	DO NOT WRITE IN THIS SPACE
	Entered By:
	Approval/Denial By:

HAVE YOU AT **ANY** TIME BEEN ARRESTED OR RECEIVED A CITATION FOR ANY OFFENSE?
☐ YES   ☐ NO
(WITH THE EXCEPTION OF SPEEDING AND PARKING VIOLATIONS) IF YES, LIST THE ARREST AND THE CITATIONS

YEAR	CITY AND STATE	OFFENSE CHARGED WITH	LENGTH OF SENTENCE/FINE

NOTE: COMPLETE REVERSE SIDE BEFORE SIGNING

I HEREBY CERTIFY THAT THE ABOVE INFORMATION
IS TRUE AND CORRECT TO THE BEST OF MY ABILITY

X _____
APPLICANT'S SIGNATURE

LVMPD TSD 18 - B (REV. 2-00)

DO NOT DUPLICATE

FALSE INFORMATION WILL CAUSE
REVOCATION OR DENIAL OF THIS APPLICATION

X _____
SIGNATURE OF EMPLOYER

Date: _____

PRINTED NAME OF EMPLOYER SIGNING

When it's Okay to be Fingerprinted

Conversely, this is why it is fine to be fingerprinted under the new identity if you have never previously been fingerprinted. In fact, this is a strategy some people living under a new identity follow to harden the new identity. Fingerprints are considered to be absolute identification, so once an individual has been fingerprinted under a name, the law will presume that identity to be the true identity. The first name you give when you are fingerprinted becomes your real name.

Once again, I cannot overemphasize this fact. If you have previously been arrested and fingerprinted under your real name, you must avoid any situation where fingerprinting is done as part of a pre-employment screening. It is just a matter of time before you are exposed and face, at the very least, being fired, and at the worst, jail or other serious legal problems. Some employers after discovering an imposter months later via fingerprints, sue the hapless individual for all of the salary they had been paid plus damages. Companies will not go easy on you if you are detected, so avoid the risk.

The Employment Application

Most employment application forms for lower-level jobs are very typical where a passive background check is required. They request basic personal information, as well as pointed questions about criminal convictions. The application asks if you have ever been convicted of a felony, and also asks if you agree to be tested for drugs prior to employment.

Some applications will have a separate release form, which includes your name, Social Security number and signature, allowing the employer to access your credit report. Most employers are very careful about checking the financial backgrounds of their employees to reduce the chance of employee theft of merchandise and from the cash register.

Although these forms seem formidable, a correctly constructed new identity can defeat nearly all passive investigations. In later chapters we will examine what steps need to be taken to successfully pass this level of screening. First, however, we need to look at the active investigation, to learn why those who are living under a new identity must avoid it.

CHAPTER NINE

Active Investigations

If the goal of the passive investigation is merely to determine that the job applicant is not a "bad guy," the goal of the active investigation is to determine that you really are a good guy. In the first, the lack of negative or contradictory information is considered affirmation of the facts presented. The active investigation follows a completely different route. The goal of the active investigator is to confirm every piece of factual data the applicant reveals about himself, and then to go on a fishing expedition to turn up any credible sources of negative data the applicant might not have revealed. At the highest level, an active investigation should be able to establish the general life history of an individual, all the way back to grade school.

When to Expect an Active Investigation

Only a few organizations carry out full-scale active investigations. The primary deterrent is the very high cost involved. Performing one of these investigations can easily run into many thousands of dollars and consume many hours of an investigator's time. As a result, they are usually only performed by federal government agencies when hiring for a higher-level management position, a position that allows access to sensitive or classified information, a position in federal law enforcement agencies, anything requiring a security clearance from the defense department, or for a contractor working for the defense department.

The security screening performed by most local and state law enforcement agencies, state and local governments, and even school districts, is almost always a passive investigation — with the addition of fingerprints — which was covered in the previous chapter. People who will perform at executive-level positions, or have control of large sums of money, may also face an active investigation.

The Paperwork

The first indication of an active investigation is the sheer amount of detailed information that is requested. The employment history for the last fifteen years is commonly requested, along with a geographical listing of all addresses lived at over the same or even longer, period of time. Copies of the job applicant's academic transcripts are also frequently requested, along with photocopies of the current driver's license, Social Security number, and birth certificate.

The paperwork requests that the applicant provide the names, addresses, and telephone numbers of many different people who can act as references. Very specifically, some are work-related, others will be nonwork-related. A complete educational history is required. On each part of this paperwork, the applicant is asked for dates and places.

Personal History Statement

A section of paperwork, known formally as a personal history or PHS, asks about legal matters. The applicant is asked to disclose the details of all marriages and divorces: when and where any marriage and any subsequent divorce took place, and to whom. The applicant is also asked about the citizenship status of himself and his spouse. The PHS asks if the applicant is subject to any current lawsuits or is in bankruptcy. He is also asked if he has ever filed for bankruptcy relief in the past, or has had a judgment or garnishment action taken against him. If the answers to any of these questions are yes, a full explanation must be provided.

The Searches

Once all the paperwork has been completed, the investigator begins a multipart process. The first step is the national agency check, which is the heart and soul of the passive investigation. This check will serve to eliminate, quickly and cheaply, anyone with a criminal record who would not qualify for the position. The next phase begins the process of confirming the accuracy of documents, such as driver's licenses, birth certificates, etc.

The investigator sends a request to the state department of motor vehicles asking for a copy of the driving record matching the license number. This confirms that the license presented is authentic, that the applicant has a satisfactory driving record, and most importantly, will tell the investigator other important information including:

- ☐ When the license was first issued?

- ☐ Was this license issued in exchange for a license from another state? If so, they will order a copy of the driving record from that state.

- ☐ Was the applicant older when the license was obtained?

This data can point the investigator to look for information in other states and locations the applicant may have attempted to obscure by carefully creating gaps in the background statement.

The investigator calls the university or college claimed on the PHS and requests verification of the degree. In a passive investigation, this would be the extent of the follow-up. In an active investigation, the investigator then writes or calls the registrar's office at the school and orders a copy of the transcript, for which the applicant will have signed a transcript release form. When the transcript arrives from the school, the investigator compares it against the copy previously given him by the applicant. Inflating grades, or adding courses altogether, is not uncommon. It may very well be true that the applicant has a degree in molecular biology from Princeton, but it might turn out that he just barely graduated with a C- average.

The Credit Report

The investigator also orders a copy of the full credit report, not just a header printout. We need to distinguish between the two types of data an investigator extracts from a credit bureau file on the applicant.

The Header. Credit reports are divided into three main sections. The section at the top is known as the "header." The header contains the following information:

☐ Full name

☐ Social Security number

☐ Birth date

☐ Current address

☐ Previous two addresses

☐ Employer

☐ Telephone number

Header data is considered public record, meaning that it is legal for anyone to access this information. All of the credit bureaus sell header searches to investigation companies and information brokerages. When you see an advertisement for a website that says they can locate lost friends or relatives or find out personal data about your neighbor, much of this information comes from credit report header information.

Credit History. The second part of the credit report contains the actual credit history. This is an accounting of all of the creditors this particular individual does business with. This section will contain the following data:

☐ Name of creditor

☐ Account number

☐ Type of account (credit card, loan account, etc.)

☐ Current balance

☐ Credit limit

☐ Highest balance

☐ Account rating of payment history

Fair Credit Reporting Act. This part of the credit report is the only part that is privacy-protected under the Fair Credit Reporting Act. To access this data, the potential employer must have a signed release from the applicant. This is why a formal credit report release form is included with almost all job applications. Though some passive investigation employers and some landlords may want the entire report, most of the time they only want the header information and the public record data — bankruptcies, liens, etc. The reality is that usually only a job requiring an active investigation involves the full credit report being requested. The investigator discerns from this part of the credit report how responsible the applicant is with managing his money. If the investigator notices numerous accounts with late payments or over-the-limit status, the applicant may well be asked to explain himself. Another consideration, particularly if the job involves access to large amounts of corporate funds, is if applicants are carrying an excessive debt load that could cause them to embezzle company money to cover their own bills.

If an investigator finds thirty open credit card accounts, all of them with very high balances, at or near the limit, red flags are raised even if all of the payments are current. An individual in this precarious position is only a small step away from financial insolvency.

Public Record and Inquiry Data. The last part of the credit report contains public record information and inquiry data. Public record information includes items such as bankruptcy filings, civil liens, and judgments filed against the applicant. The investigator is looking for lack of entries on this part of the report. A bankruptcy or civil lien will not result in the applicant being automatically disqualified from further consideration, if the applicant disclosed these adverse items on the personal history statement and explained what brought them about. Some people are forced into bankruptcy because of medical bills or long-term unemployment. People can become the subject of a lawsuit because they were involved in an accident or a legitimate business dispute. In general, so long as the bankruptcy was discharged by the court and is considered to be well in the past, it will not kill the applicant's chances. The same is true of a lien or judgment. What will kill an applicant's chances is a pattern of judgments over many years. This could be an indication of irresponsibility.

The inquiry section, which is at the very end of the credit report, lists everyone who has requested a copy of the credit report over the last year to eighteen months. If XYZ Bank requested a copy of this credit report nine months previously, the XYZ Bank name, subscriber code, and date of request are listed. Note, however, that requests for header information only do not cause any entry to be made on the credit report inquiry section. The investigator is interested in seeing who else has requested a copy of your credit report. This may point to other areas of focus for the investigation.

Additional Financial Background

Depending on the level and type of clearance required, additional financial investigating may be conducted. The primary goal of this additional financial backgrounding will be to determine if there are any financial skeletons in the closet. The most important of these would be someone who is living beyond his or her means, and it cannot be explained.

The investigator performs an asset check and determines the value of any house, other property, and vehicles owned, and the outstanding loan amounts against them. Educated guesses can be made about family expenses. If the applicant has two teen-aged children who both go to pricey private schools, this expense is calculated and compared against that of the family income. If the apparent lifestyle seems out of range for the income earned, the applicant may be asked for an explanation. Perhaps the applicant's parents are helping pay for their grandchildrens' schooling or the applicant has a part-time, income-producing hobby, such as writing, that provides additional income. If the applicant indicates a secondary source of support such as this, the investigator requests permission to verify it with the grandparents, for example, or requests the 1099 from the publisher or other income payer.

Name Verification

The investigator confirms that the applicant's birth certificate is real by writing to the vital statistics agency where the certificate was issued and requesting a copy for himself. He then notes if the exact name on the birth certificate matches that used on other documents obtained from the applicant. Minor changes, such as using Bill for William, are noted. Bigger changes are brought to the attention of the applicant, who is asked for an explanation.

In the case of a married woman who has stopped using her maiden name, the good investigator will run a "parallel" track investigation for additional records in the maiden name in the years after marriage. Many female applicants with spotty backgrounds have attempted to jettison them by using their married name, and omitting any references to their maiden name. Thus, record checks under the married name come back clean, because the negative records are all listed under the maiden name.

The fingerprint check is performed concurrently. Fingerprint cards are matched against the state database in each state where the applicant has had a previous residence, and a set is matched against the central fingerprint file maintained by the FBI. If the applicant has said he was never fingerprinted, then the card coming back should be the one which was submitted and has now created a new file in the database. If there is already an existing fingerprint card, it means that the applicant either lied or forgot he had been fingerprinted previously — possibly for a noncriminal reason, such as military service.

Personal History Verification

At this point in the active investigation, much has been learned about the applicant. It is very likely he is who he says he is, and his background and character are as he has maintained. If the investigation was stopped at this point, it would be quite possible for a well-constructed false identity to slip through this amount of screening. But the investigation is not over, and the next phase will expose all but one type of fake identity. In this phase of the active investigation, the investigator seeks to create a constellation of people who have known or interacted with the applicant back to high school, or even further, in some cases. Consider how this happens.

There are very few people most of us have known our entire life. The reality is that at different times in your life, you have some very good friends, and then you drift apart later, maybe only maintaining sporadic contact. There might be two or three people you can say you have kept in relatively close contact with over a lifetime who are not relatives. In college, there is the college roommate. At your first real job outside of college, there was your best buddy in the office down the hall, and later, the neighbor next door from where you bought your first house.

Checking Past Contacts

The active investigator now starts working backwards in time from the present, putting together this constellation of people who have intersected with your life over the years. They interview these people, often in person, and ask them if they remember you. Most importantly, they ask them about when they first met you and how they met you. This information is entered into a log and plotted on a timeline.

If the applicant is 40 years old, and the investigator decides to go back to the time he graduated from high school — which is typical — this timeline will reflect various people who have known the applicant, and then heard less from him. Also, these differing groups of people will overlap for some of the time periods. This is what the investigator will find with a real identity and with someone who has been truthful about his past. The final element of the investigation is frequently a visit to the old high school and a quick talk with a teacher who is still there from when the applicant was a student, or if this is no longer possible, a look at the yearbook photograph will confirm the applicant's presence.

Only now can the investigation be closed, and the investigator satisfied that the applicant is really who he claims to be. This final phase also explains why nearly any constructed identity will be detected.

The Danger of a New Identity

No matter how well a fake identity is documented, it had to be created at a certain point in time. Before this date of creation, there are records and, most importantly, no one who can say they knew the individual. There will be a definite "break" where all records regarding this fictitious person simply stop. A definite break like this is a telltale sign to an investigator that the identity might be fictitious.

For example, let us assume that the person created the new identity in 1985. The new-identity creator has been very careful, obtaining a driver's license, voter registration documents, employment history, credit cards, etc. He also has many friends who have known him over the many intervening years. But one hard fact remains. None of these people will have known the applicant before 1985, and there will be no public records in existence before then. This, in a nutshell is why anyone living under a created identity must avoid the full-blown active investigation. Thankfully, these are rarely conducted.

CHAPTER TEN

Credit Bureau Screening

We have seen that many employers use the credit report as a screening tool to determine if a job applicant makes it to the level of consideration. This can take either the form of requesting the full credit report or just the header data. Some companies have so automated the process that the contents of the credit or credit header screening will determine the outcome for the applicant. A number of nationwide electronic retailers have even set up in-store kiosks and the job applicant answers some questions via telephone or on a computer screen. At the end of the interview, the computer then calls the credit bureau and accesses the credit report information of the job applicant. If the credit data confirms and the applicant's responses to the questions is positive, an offer of employment may be made right then and there.

It is crucial, therefore, that the person seeking employment via a new identity understands how to defeat, or at least manipulate, the credit bureaus so that the answers it returns to the employer are favorable. The key to understanding how to manipulate credit bureau files is to realize that the primary file retrieval tool used by the credit bureaus is the Social Security number. Glance at any employment application. You will notice that the only data requested on the credit report release form aside from the name, is the Social Security number. A file can be retrieved from all three credit bureaus by using only a Social Security number.

Creating a Social Security Number

It is necessary to understand how Social Security numbers are created, because the new-identity user must initially use a made-up Social Security number until a real number can be obtained. If this number is made up correctly, it will create the background you need. If this is done wrong, your new identity can be exposed with the simplest of background checks.

The key is to create a Social Security number that is potentially valid, but does not yet belong to anyone now in the credit bureau system. This has become easier to do because the government is encouraging the parents of newborn infants to obtain Social Security numbers. Most parents do so, because if they want to claim child-care expenses as a tax deduction, the infant must have a Social Security number. Contrast this with the situation 25 years ago, when most people got their Social Security numbers when they took a first job as a teenager or went off to college. This means there are millions of recently issued Social Security numbers that are not yet in the credit bureau files, and will not be for many years.

Area Numbers

The Social Security number consists of three parts. The first three digits are known as area numbers and range from 001 to 772. These numbers are assigned based on the mailing address of the applicant. Each state is assigned certain blocks of area numbers. In Appendix 2 is a reprint of a Social Security Administration document showing which area numbers are assigned to each state. So the first step in creating a background is to create a Social Security number from a state where you want to have a background. This can be done by picking an area number that is assigned to the state you desire.

Group Numbers

This then leads us to the middle two digits of the Social Security number. These middle two digits are known as group numbers, and in many ways, these are the most important digits in the number.

Group numbers range from 01 to 99. These numbers can tell a knowledgeable individual — or a computer — if the Social Security number presented is potentially valid, or would have been issued to the applicant. If the group number is manipulated correctly, the job seeker can easily penetrate the credit bureau database and create a good file.

The very first group numbers assigned to a given are the odd groups under 10. So, take the state of Wyoming. The area number assigned to Wyoming is 520. All Social Security numbers issued to people in Wyoming start with 520, and the very first number assigned was 520-01-0001. This explains the last four digits, which are called serial numbers. These numbers range from 0001 to 9999. The second Social Security number issued in Wyoming would be 520-01-0002. These numbers continued in sequential order until 520-01-9999 was assigned. The number issued after 520-01-9999 would be 520-03-0001, and the same process was repeated.

When 520-09-9999 is assigned, the Social Security Administration will then began issuing the even group numbers from 10 through 98. So the next Social Security number issued in Wyoming after 520-09-9999 would be 520-10-0001. After the even group numbers between 10 and 98 were assigned, then the even group numbers less than 10 were assigned, and then they began assigning the odd group numbers between 11 and 99. So the pattern is odd, even, even, and odd. After all these numbers are assigned, new area numbers will be allocated to Wyoming. This is why some large population states are assigned many different area numbers.

Social Security started issuing numbers to people in 1935, so it is clear that someone with a very low group number from an original issue area number must be very old or they are lying. Consider the Wyoming example. Because of its sparse population, Wyoming has only one area number assigned to it. Anyone claiming a 01 to 99 group number from Wyoming had better be pretty old. Credit bureau computers are programmed to catch improbable Social Security numbers by checking the year of issuance against the birth date of the subject, if available.

In the same way, credit bureau computers can also detect Social Security numbers that could not have been issued yet or are impossible combinations. Also in Appendix 2 is a reprint from the Social Security Administration of the highest group numbers assigned to each area as of May 1, 2002. This information is provided to credit bureaus and is used in their database. If someone attempts to retrieve a file with an invalid number, a warning will be placed across the credit report stating that the Social Security number is out of range or not yet issued.

The Death Claim

Another caution involves Social Security numbers that have had a death claim paid against them. The Social Security Administration maintains the Social Security Death Index, or SSDI. If the relatives claim the death benefit, the Social Security Administration places the decedent's name, Social Security number, birth date and place of death into this database (see below). This database is updated quarterly and is widely used by credit bureaus. If someone applies for credit using a Social Security number that has had a death claim filed against it, a warning will flash on the credit report.

This is an example from Ancestry.com — Social Security Death Index Search Results

<u>**Search Results Provided By**</u>   The No. 1 Source for Family History online *Ancestry.com*

Database: Social Security Death Index

<u>**Viewing records 11-13 of 13**</u>   <u>April 8, 2002 1:59 AM</u>

ROBERT L DECKER   (Request Information (SS-5)

SSN	483-26-4975	**Residence:**	50703 Waterloo, Black Hawk, IA
Born	27 Aug 1928	**Last Benefit:**	
Died	16 Aug 1993	**Issued:**	IA (Before 1951)

ROBERT DECKER   (Request Information (SS-5)

SSN	484-44-8244	**Residence:**	52772 Tipton, Cedar, IA
Born	8 Sep 1908	**Last Benefit:**	
Died	29 Jan 1993	**Issued:**	IA (1955)

RUTH H DECKER   (Request Information SS-5)

SSN	485-24-6170	**Residence:**	51301 Spencer, Clay, IA
Born	22 Nov 1901	**Last Benefit:**	
Died	Sep 1993	**Issued:**	IA (Before 1951)

Checking the Numbers

The applicant needs to make up a Social Security number that will reflect the background he wishes to portray, is potentially valid but not yet assigned to anyone with a credit file and which has not been the subject of a death claim. This is not difficult to do. The first step is to use the lists provided in the Appendix to construct a recent-issue Social Security number from the desired state. A list of three potential numbers should be made up. Once these numbers have been made up, the first check should be to make sure there has been no death claim filed. This can be done at no cost over the Internet.

The website www.Ancestry.com has a link to a relatively recent update of the Social Security Death Index. Enter the three numbers into this database and see if anything is returned. If nothing comes back, all three numbers are good possibilities.

The next step is to verify that no one is using these numbers who is already in the credit bureau system. This is also easy to do, and will cost you around $50 per number. There are numerous companies, known as information brokers, who package and resell credit bureau header data — the part that is public record and available to anyone. You can purchase a Social Security number sweep and they will then search all three credit bureaus for any information. If this search comes back with a "no record found," it means these numbers are ideal for your purposes. A list of information brokers is given in Appendix 2. The important thing is to make sure that the Social Security sweep is performed on all three credit bureau systems, not just one.

Address and Credit Bureau Screenings

When credit bureaus use the Social Security number as a screening device, and no current record is found with the given Social Security number, a new file is created. If this Social Security number is potentially valid, and neither belongs to someone else already in the system nor is the subject of a death claim, none of the Social Security warning programs are triggered.

Unfortunately, this is only half of the battle. The addresses used on the credit report are also critical. Credit bureau computer systems are programmed to recognize addresses that are not residential, or belong to mail drops, check-cashing agencies, and answering services. Therefore, it is necessary for the person living under a new identity to preplan what addresses will be used on employment paperwork, to prevent the credit report or header data throwing up a warning about the address. Luckily, there are techniques that can be used to circumvent this problem.

Acquiring a Good Address

It will be necessary to obtain a good address for the paperwork one needs when creating a new identity. A post office box is frequently not acceptable as a residential address, because you may not really reside at that location. Your best choices are either a commercial mail-forwarding service or a secretarial/office-rental service.

The benefit of these services is that you get a street address. Many of the mail-receiving services are located in residential areas, so your address will appear to be in a part of town where people live, not an industrial area. All mail-receiving services are required to comply with certain U.S. postal service requirements. One of these is the official paperwork that must be completed and kept on file. This is known as PS Form 1583, and it is reproduced at the end of this chapter.

The PS-1583. This form requires that the mail-forwarding service obtain two pieces of identification from you, along with your true residential address. A copy of this form is retained at the business, usually with a copy of the customer's identification and the signed original is sent to the local postmaster. There was a time when a mail-receiving service could avoid using this form, but it is now mandatory unless the company exploits a loophole mentioned below.

As a practical matter, you will have no trouble with this paper work if you use a good-quality fake ID. Most mail-drop operators are just interested in making a profit, and so long as you are not conducting fraud or running child pornography through their business, they could care less. In general, there is no verification of any of the data on this form.

The loophole that allows you to avoid using this form involves the secretarial or office-rental service. Because the receiving of mail is only a small part of their business, they are not required to use this form. I recommend using one of these services because, as a second benefit, most of them are not flagged in credit bureau computers.

Ghost Address. There is a way to get the benefit of having a legitimate street address of a real house or apartment, and still receive your mail at a mail drop. This is called the "ghost address" technique. First, locate an apartment complex in a nice area of town. Pick a large complex, not a rattrap, but not super-expensive. Apartment complexes like this have people moving in and out all the time. It is even better if they have a mailroom and the postal carrier simply delivers everyone's mail to a mailroom.

Write down the address and pick an apartment number. This will now be your new address of record on official paperwork. The next step is to file a change of address card. The address to forward from will be the address of this apartment complex. The address the mail will be sent to will be the address of the mail drop or secretarial service.

At the end of the chapter we have reproduced the postal change of address card, PS Form 3575. You might be wondering if the mail carrier will realize that I never lived at the apartment address? Not likely. In a small town, or if you were forwarding from a single-family residence, there is a good chance your ruse will be detected. In a large city apartment complex, people are so transient that your mail-forwarding order is just one of many.

Many times you need to make up two previous addresses. The same method can be used. Simply look under Apartments in the Yellow Pages in the city you want to have had a former address in, or search on the Internet. You can create legitimate sounding addresses anywhere with no problem via this technique.

PS Form 1583

United States Postal Service

Application for Delivery of Mail Through Agent
See Privacy Act Statement on Reverse

	1. Date

In consideration of delivery of my or our (firm) mail to the agent named below, the addressee and agent agree: (1) the addressee or the agent must not file a change of address order with the Postal Service upon termination of the agency relationship; (2) the transfer of my or our (firm) mail to another address is the responsibility of the agent; (3) all mail delivered to the agency under this authorization must be prepaid with new postage when redeposited in the mails; (4) upon request the agent must provide to the Postal Service all addresses to which the agency transfers mail; and (5) when any information required on this form changes or becomes obsolete, the addressee(s) must file a revised application with the Commercial Mail Receiving Agency (CMRA).

NOTE: The applicant must execute this form in duplicate in the presence of the agent, his or her authorized employee, or a notary public. The agent provides the original completed signed Form 1583 to the Postal Service and retains a duplicate completed signed copy at the CMRA business location. The CMRA copy of Form 1583 must at all times be available for examination by the postmaster (or designee) and the Postal Inspection Service. The addressee and the agent agree to comply with all applicable postal rules and regulations relative to delivery of mail through an agent. Failure to comply will subject the agency to withholding of mail from delivery until corrective action is taken.

This application may be subject to verification procedures by the Postal Service to confirm that the applicant resides or conducts business at the home or business address listed in boxes 8 or 11, and that the identification listed in box 9 is valid.

2. Name in Which Applicant's Mail Will Be Received for Delivery to Agent. (Complete a separate Form 1583 for EACH applicant. Spouses may complete and sign one Form 1583. Two items of valid identification apply to each spouse. Include dissimilar information for either spouse in appropriate box.)

3. Address to Be Used for Delivery Including ZIP + 4

4. Applicant Authorizes Delivery to and in Care of (Name, address, and ZIP Code of agent)

5. Will This Delivery Address Be Used for Soliciting or Doing Business With the Public? (Check one) ☐ Yes ☐ No

7. Name of Applicant

6. This Authorization Is Extended to Include Restricted Delivery Mail for the Undersigned(s)

8. Home Address (Number, street, city, state, and ZIP Code)

9. Two Types of Identification are Required. One Must Contain a Photograph of the Addressee(s). Agent Must Write in Identifying Information. Subject to Verification.
a.
b.

Telephone Number (   )

10. Name of Firm or Corporation

11. Business Address (Number, street, city, state and ZIP Code)

Acceptable identification includes: driver's license; armed forces, government, or recognized corporate identification card; passport or alien registration card or other credential showing the applicant's signature and a serial number or similar information that is traceable to the bearer. A photocopy of your identification may be retained by agent for verification.

Telephone Number (   )

12. Kind of Business

13. If Applicant Is a Firm, Name Each Member Whose Mail Is to Be Delivered. (All names listed must have verifiable identification. A guardian must list the names and ages of minors receiving mail at their delivery address.)

14. If a CORPORATION, Give Names and Addresses of Its Officers

15. If Business Name of The Address (Corporation or Trade Name) Has Been Registered, Give Name of County and State, and Date of Registration.

Warning: The furnishing of false or misleading information on this form or omission of material information may result in criminal sanctions (including fines and imprisonment) and/or civil sanctions (including multiple damages and civil penalties). (18 U.S.C. 1001)

16. Signature of Agent/Notary Public

17. Signature of Applicant (If firm or corporation, application must be signed by officer. Show title.)

PS Form **1583**, March 1999

This form on Internet at www.usps.com

PS Form 3575

OFFICIAL MAIL FORWARDING CHANGE OF ADDRESS FORM

U.S. Postal Service
CHANGE OF ADDRESS ORDER

Instructions: Complete Items 1 thru 10. You must SIGN Item 9. Please PRINT all other items including address on face of card.

OFFICIAL USE ONLY
Zone/Route ID No.

1. Change of Address for: (See instruction #1 above)
☐ Individual   ☐ Entire Family   ☐ Business

2. Start Date: Month Day Year

Date Entered on Form 3982
M M D D Y Y

3. Is This Move Temporary? (Check one)
☐ No   ☐ Yes, Fill in ▶
4. If TEMPORARY move, print date to discontinue forwarding: Month Day Year

Expiration Date
M M D D Y Y

5. Print Last Name (include Jr., Sr., etc.) or Name of Business (If more than one, use separate form for each).

Clerk/Carrier Endorsement

6. Print First Name (or Initial) and Middle Name (or Initial). Leave blank if for a business.

7a. **For Puerto Rico Only:** If OLD mailing address is in Puerto Rico, print urbanization name, if appropriate.

7b. Print **OLD** mailing address: House/Building Number and Street Name (include St., Ave., Rd., Ct., etc.).

Apt./Suite No.   or   PO Box No.   or ☐RR/ ☐HCR (Check one)   RR/HCR Box No.

City   State   ZIP Code   ZIP+4

8a. **For Puerto Rico Only:** If NEW mailing address is in Puerto Rico, print urbanization name, if appropriate.

8b. Print **NEW** mailing address: House/Building Number and Street Name (include St., Ave., Rd., Ct., etc.).

Apt./Suite No.   or   ☐ PO Box No. / ☐ PMB No. (Check one)   or ☐RR/ ☐HCR   ☐PMB No./☐RR/HCR Box No.

City   State   ZIP Code   ZIP+4

9. Sign and Print Name (see conditions on reverse)
Sign:
Print:

10. Date Signed: Month Day Year

OFFICIAL USE ONLY
Verification Endorsement

PS FORM 3575, May 2002   See **http://www.moversguide.com** for more information.   0052

CHAPTER ELEVEN

Create an Employment History

With the techniques of the previous chapter, you can now safely pass the screening that employers will do via credit bureaus. In many cases, this is all of the screening done, and an offer of employment will be made soon after. This will frequently be the case in retail employment when unemployment rates are low, and these businesses have a difficult time locating new workers. Many companies, however, will want to contact previous employers. Most of the time, they will be content with just contacting the last employer, but some companies have different policies.

Some will want to contact all employers over a given time period, say, ten years. This approach is very common with firms that do aerospace work, or any airline, especially in light of the terrorist attacks. Some companies have a policy that requires them to check the last three employers, regardless of the time period. Of course, if the applicant has only two previous employers, as with a younger adult or teenager, this is acceptable.

In the context of an overall background investigation, it is important not only that your employment history be verifiable, but that it reflects the background you wish to portray. If your new identity includes a past in Oregon, for example, then you should have previous employment references from there. Nothing raises red flags faster than mismatches or unexplained differences between the personal background and the employment background.

Constructing a Background

The first step is to decide where you want your past to come from. Much of this detail should have been addressed when creating your new identity, but as a general rule, you should only create a past history for yourself that is plausible and believable. If you are Mexican-American and have a strong accent, creating a past for yourself as a farmhand in North Dakota who is now trying his hand in the big city will raise more questions than it answers.

Never pick a place as a background which you know nothing about or do not have the ability to learn about. If your cover story is that you are from Seattle, you had better know enough about Seattle to convince someone who is from there that you actually lived there. America is a highly mobile society and the human resources screener or a potential boss might have just come from Seattle a few years earlier. At a minimum you should be familiar with the general layout of the city, special or notable civic attractions, have an idea of where major landmarks are, know the names of the local pro and college sports teams, know what type of weather the place has, and the primary industries and employers. A complete "must-know" checklist appears in Appendix 2.

The good news is that now, with the easy availability of the Internet, you can learn all of this and much more right from a computer terminal in your own home or public library. Simply enter the name of your desired city into any search engine and you will be deluged with more information than you can possibly learn. The important thing is to not rush this learning process; if you do a slipshod job, it will come back to haunt you later. By spending the time necessary to truly learn the details of your new background, you will be more confident and sure of yourself when you are playing the role of being a native of some place you might never have stepped foot in.

The Benefits of Distance

The more distance between where you are going to and where your background is from, the better. This minimizes the possibility that someone will know that the employment references you create are fabricated and not those of genuine businesses. With this exception, the employment references you create will be verifiable and enable you to pass by most pre-employment screening.

Backstop Your History

Most of the time previous employment is verified via a telephone call to the previous employer listed on the employment application. In some instances, a letter will be sent asking for a reference. In both cases, due to legal reasons, the gist of the conversation or letter will focus on two questions. The first will be whether the applicant was, in fact, an employee at the company in the capacity and during the time period indicated? The second will be, "Would this person be eligible for rehire?"

The questions are phrased this way because former employees have successfully sued employers if they told a prospective employer that the former employee was lousy or lazy. The phrasing keeps the discussion on factual terms only: either the person did or did not work at the company during the dates indicated and either they would or wouldn't be eligible for rehire. Most employers will not say anything more than this and will not confirm details such as previous salary.

The good news in all this is that the employment reference system can be easily manipulated if you are willing to take the time to build and backstop a solid employment history. I recommend that two previous employers be created. The first previous employer is your primary previous employment reference. This reference should be completely backstopped, and you should have worked there at least five years. The second employer need only be partially backstopped, but enough to be verified.

Keep in mind what we said about geographic separation between the old and the new. America is a very large nation, but some professions and fields are relatively small. Hence, you are better off making your previous employment in an entirely different line of work than what you want to do in the new location, particularly if the desired area of employment is rather small or specialized. This avoids the small chance of someone knowing that your former employer does not exist.

Creating an Employer

The first step in building an employment reference is to come up with a company name. Do not use any variation of your own name and avoid those of real companies, especially nationwide businesses. Come up with a list of about ten different names, then do a nationwide telephone directory search to see if any of them are already listed. This is easily done via the Internet. Simply go to one of the nationwide "find a business" pages and plug in the name. If you find matches, a small change in the name of the corporation will often be enough to avoid any conflicts with a real business. Of course, our "company" will only serve one purpose, and aside from this, it will have a very low profile.

Once you have a company name, you need to set up a mailing address and telephone number. This is best done with a high-end secretarial service, one that will also provide a telephone number. Expect to pay around $100 for what is frequently known as a company "identity" package. For this fee you will receive a corporate street address, mail handling, and frequently a telephone number. For an added monthly fee you can arrange to have this telephone number listed with directory assistance and in the local telephone book. Do so. You now have a working company address and telephone number. You can have a recorded voice-mail message or arrange to have a live operator answer the number during office hours.

The next step is to register the domain name of the company. All legitimate businesses have a Web site and yours should be no different. For less than $100 you can register the corporate domain with Network Solutions or a competitor, and then arrange to set up a bare bones Web site with a hosting service. By making the corporate description somewhat nebulous — consulting or something similar — you can avoid having to be too specific on your Web site. It also will give you flexibility when describing your previous job title.

Incorporation

The next step is to make this cover company a real business entity by incorporating it. I recommend you incorporate the firm in Nevada. Nevada has the least burdensome incorporation requirements of all the states, and it can be done relatively cheaply. Nevada also requires very little information about the corporate directors, so they can be fictitious without the state knowing any different. Finally, Nevada does not tax corporations, which eliminates a paperwork headache.

Why incorporate? Because now your cover company will have a real Employer Identification Number issued by the IRS and it is now a real, legally constituted entity. This means your company can now issue all the paperwork "real" corporations do: W-2 forms, 1099 forms, statements of earnings, corporate reference letters, etc.

There are many excellent incorporation services one can use. At a minimum, you will want to purchase an incorporation package that includes a corporate mailing address for legal service and the provision of the corporate seal and documents. It is necessary to have a mailing address for legal service within the state of Nevada. On your corporate letterhead this address will be listed as your headquarters and the address in your "background" city will be listed as a branch office.

Creating Company Detritus

Once this is done, you will need to get corporate letterheads printed. Go to a copy shop or a business center, and they will help you pick out a corporate logo and letterhead. Do not skimp. Purchase high-quality paper and envelopes that would impress the recipient. Consider the correspondence you have received from corporations in the past. It is almost always on high-quality paper; and yours should be as well.

Your incorporation service should have arranged with the IRS to obtain an Employer Identification Number. This will allow you to generate W-2 forms and other documents that can be used as proof of income or earnings. Some employers may wish to see proof of your previous salary, or you might need a payroll stub as a secondary proof of identification for some purpose. You can now manufacture these at will. These documents can be useful when renting an apartment if the rental agency wants proof of income, or at a motor vehicle department were proof of your Social Security number is required. They can also be used to establish proof of residency.

Job References

You are now in a position to write yourself an excellent job reference. In general, these reference letters should simply verify the dates of your former employment, state the capacity in which you were employed, and close with the statement that you were an excellent worker and that if more information is required, the letter writer should be contacted. A letter such as this can be photocopied and included with resumes and job applications. In many instances, if a written letter of reference is included from a former employer, no further verification will take place. This is especially true of small firms or for low-level jobs.

Never claim military service. It is quite easy to document, because the form employers are supposed to accept from veterans as proof of service, the DD-214, is easily forged. But it is simply too big a risk that you will run into someone who actually served in the unit you claimed to have been in. Second, employers receive certain tax breaks and other benefits for hiring veterans, and any paperwork done on your behalf will be rejected out of the system.

The second employment reference should be constructed like the first one, with the exception that you need not go to the trouble of actually incorporating the company. For completeness, you can carry out all of the steps if you wish. The second company can be in the same city as the first, or in a different location. If it is in a different city, make sure you take the steps to familiarize yourself with this city as well.

In Appendix 3 is a reprint of an incorporation advertisement from a firm that offers this type of service. A complete listing of such services can be found on the Internet.

CHAPTER TWELVE

Create an Education History

Another problem the job seeker will confront is how to create or recreate an educational background. Once again, the key to doing this effectively is to know which kinds of records are routinely verified and which are not. The good news is that educational credentials can almost always be bluffed if you provide appropriate documentation for what is claimed and can effectively play the role of someone with your purported background. This is true, even in cases where your degree is not directly related to the job being sought. Many employers require college degrees of all workers, even if the job, such as sales, has nothing to do with a particular field. Employers have found that people with college backgrounds make better workers.

Cautions

However, be careful. If you are claiming a degree in computer Science, but your knowledge of computer programming is rudimentary, watch out. If you get a job selling cars with a fake resume that says you speak French, you had better be able to speak French when, by chance, that couple who just moved to America comes to your lot to buy a car. Your sales manager will be beaming when he sends them straight to you to close the deal. Five minutes later you will be on the street, exposed as a fraud when not one word of French escapes your lips.

So, we start this chapter with what not to do. Do not claim skills you do not have, no matter how expedient it may seem. It will get you in trouble later on, in some way you did not expect.

Diploma Mills

The second no-no is purchasing a degree from what are known as diploma mills. You see advertisements for these "institutions of higher learning" on the Internet as well as in national publications such as *USA Today*. These need to be avoided because, as one book described it, using a degree from one of these schools is like putting a "time bomb" in your resume.

People are caught using diploma mill degrees because the schools must advertise to stay in business. A new diploma mill gets set up, starts advertising, and then thousands of people purchase degrees from it. Most of these customers never get caught, at least not right away, but then someone gets into trouble with one of these purchased sheepskins and the school becomes front-page news. If criminal laws have been violated, the list of "graduates" may be made known to the police and you could find yourself the recipient of some attention from law enforcement agencies.

If your employer finds out your degree is from a diploma mill, you might not only be fired, but also sued for civil fraud and have to pay back any wages you received, plus damages, plus lawyer fees. Your reputation, and hence the value of your new identity, will have been destroyed.

How do you know if a school is a diploma mill? There are some definite warning signs. If a school offers to sell you a degree outright for a set price, with little or no work, that is a good indication that it is a diploma mill. A legitimate school will want to know about your background and will have definite requirements that must be met before a degree will be awarded. If a school offers to backdate your diploma, that is another sign of a degree mill.

A flashy Web site and high-quality advertising material are no guarantee of a school's legitimacy. The Internet has created an entirely new generation of diploma mills, many based in foreign countries. Complete coverage of diploma mills and legitimate schools offering degrees nontraditionally can be found in the Recommended Reading. The discussion here will focus on two techniques that can be used to obtain a job until real educational credentials can be obtained.

The High School Diploma or GED

First, high school diplomas are rarely checked out. It is automatically assumed that you have a high school diploma and most employers do not even bother to verify this. In a rare instance, one might ask to see a copy of the high school diploma or grade transcript. It is easy to obtain a real high school diploma via the GED program. The GED will give you a legitimate high school diploma that is readily accepted by all employers and many colleges. Information on where and how to take the examinations is available from any school district office or college counselor. Review manuals can be purchased at bookstores nationwide. As a practical matter, you can claim graduation from whatever high school you want and it will be accepted at face value.

As always there are a few caveats. Make the high school far away from where you are seeking employment. Use the Internet and get some level of familiarity with your "alma mater," just in case someone at your new place of employment actually went to your school. Also, do not choose super-exclusive or high-profile schools for your old high school. Avoid Beverly Hills High School, for example. More than a few have been exposed after claiming such an exclusive pedigree. Make yourself just another nameless, faceless graduate of a large, urban high school.

College Degrees

College degrees are another matter. Most employers will want some verification of the degree. Unless it is an active investigation, this can be provided by the applicant himself. Most employers are not interested in seeing a copy of the actual degree, but want to see the transcript. The transcript is the true document that indicates when the school was attended, what courses were taken, the grades and credit received, and finally, what degree, if any, the school has conferred on the applicant. Many times, a job advertisement will require that certified copies of the academic transcript accompany the resume. When this is the case, these certified copies are accepted as proof of the degree without any further checking. If an advertisement asks for the applicant to submit official transcripts with the application, it is an excellent bet that no further verification will be made of the educational history.

Choosing a College

Therefore, it can be a powerful weapon to have the ability to turn out believable transcripts from schools of your choosing. Once again, some considerations need to be kept in mind when doing this. Do not claim medical, dental, or legal degrees. Even if you have the skills in these professions, they are so heavily regulated, you will almost certainly be exposed. The worst thing you can do is claim a medical degree without any training. Suppose you used this degree to obtain a managerial-type job. Your explanation was that you were interested in making a career change after deciding that medicine was just not for you. Months later, an accident happens at your job and someone sends for you to attend the scene until the paramedics arrive. After all, you are a doctor. You can see exactly where this little scenario is leading.

Do not claim degrees from super prestigious universities and colleges. It might seem to be a smart idea to say you are a Harvard graduate or went to Yale, but these schools have so many people who falsely claim credentials that employers tend to call them to verify directly anyone claiming a degree, even if impeccable transcripts are enclosed. Also, because of the ultra-high profile of schools like these, there is a very good chance you could run into someone who went to the school and was in the same program you "were."

Know Your College

The best bet is to make yourself a graduate of a very large, undistinguished state university, a good distance away from where you intend to seek employment. Do your homework. Use the Internet to research your alma mater and make sure that it offers the degree program you wish to claim. Once you have determined that it does, obtain a copy of the curriculum for the degree program. This is often posted on a departmental Web site. At a minimum, you should know the following facts about your new alma mater:

☐ Nickname of the school
☐ School mascot or emblem
☐ Location and approximate size
☐ Semester or quarter system

- ☐ Major sports teams
- ☐ General campus layout
- ☐ Important local knowledge of nearby area

Two easy ways to do this are to subscribe to the campus newspaper, and visit its web site regularly. The next step is to obtain a sample transcript from the school. This requires a little work, but this step is very important, because it ensures that the fake transcript you later create looks like an authentic document from the school. This is where your corporate letterhead comes in very handy.

Creating a Transcript

Run an employment ad in the school newspaper. This can be done very cheaply, and the career placement office on campus will help you do it. You might also be able to place a free flyer offering employment with your company on the bulletin boards in the student center. The job advertisement should offer employment for people with the type of qualifications you want to claim. In the ad you would offer a salary range that is about twenty percent higher than normal for entry-level workers in this profession. Request that applicants send a resume and a copy of their transcripts. Within a short time you will have plenty of sample specimens of real transcripts from the school.

Now that you have a sample, you can go about making your own forgery. Complete details on forging academic transcripts and other documents can be found in the book, *The ID Forger*. I will only make general recommendations here on some of the best practices.

Most universities use one of two types of transcripts: either a vertical type, that is, read from top to bottom; or a landscape type, where the information is displayed from left to right. Aside from this, there is a lot of commonality on the basic information. The forgery of academic transcripts can be greatly simplified if you start with the basic form most universities and colleges use and then customize it for your needs.

One place that sells the necessary forms is www.prestigious-images.com. They sell both types of transcript paper along with the computer software that allows you to place the image of the school on the paper and plot courses taken and grades received. You will, of course, be working from a real sample, so you can duplicate this precisely with the software. On the next page we have reproduced a sample of the transcript paper available for sale from this company.

A real transcript will bear a raised, embossed seal. A few schools may now issue transcripts without one, but most transcripts will have this seal. You will need to purchase a seal, although it need not be that of the school. Most people do not bother to look all that carefully at the seal itself. A seal of the state the school is located in will work just fine, especially if your university is a state school. The school seal is frequently just a modification of the state seal. State seals are available from any number of places — an office supply store can order one for you. You can also purchase one via mail from NIC Law Enforcement Supply. They also sell stamps that say useful things such as "certified copy." These can also be added to the document to enhance its authenticity. NIC Law Enforcement Supply's Web address is: www.n-i-c-inc.com.

Sample of transcript paper

THE FACE OF THIS DOCUMENT HAS A COLORED BACKGROUND ON WHITE PAPER						

ACADEMIC RECORD OF:

NAME		SS #
ADDRESS		DOB
CITY	STATE	SEX
ZIP		ADVISOR

COURSE TITLE	DIV.	CRS NO.	CREDIT ATTEMPTED	CREDIT EARNED	GRADE	GRADE POINTS

	ATT.	EARNED	G.P.	GPA	
CUM LU AND TRANSFER					
TRANSFER CREDIT	ATT.	EARNED	G.P.	GPA	

The regular grading system provides a range of grade levels indicating the student's achievement of the objectives established for a course.
A - 4 Pts. - Outstanding achievement of the educational objectives.
B - 3 Pts. - Highly satisfactory achievement of the educational objectives.
C - 2 Pts. - Adequate achievement of the educational objectives.
D - 1 Pts. - Passing, marginal achievement of the educational objectives.
F - 0 Pts. - No credit, unsatisfactory achievement.

REVERSE SIDE HAS A FLUORESCENT ARTIFICIAL WATERMARK

Degree Certificates

There might be occasions where you will actually want a degree or diploma certificate itself to photocopy or hang on a wall. You can purchase duplicates of diploma and degree certificates from companies that technically bill themselves as "document replacement services." For a fee, these services will reproduce any degree or certificate that you have "lost" or "misplaced." The legal disclaimer you sign when you purchase the document is enough to keep these people out of any trouble with the police. The best of these services is a firm known as Couch Potato Publishing, and despite their name, they produce first-class work and have been in business a long time.

Couch Potato can make an entire raft of documents and certificates: college degrees from both American and foreign schools, awards certificates, military award citations, high school diplomas, etc. You can write away for their catalog which costs about two dollars. The address is

Couch Potato Publishing
4211 Little Road, Suite 9
New Port Richey, FL 33307

Get Your Own Degree

The long-term solution is to obtain real credentials in your new name. This should be pursued even if you obtain suitable employment with your excellent forgery. Once you have real degrees, you can stop using the forgery and eliminate a weak spot in your new background. The good news is that it is now possible to earn valid, recognized degrees in many fields nontraditionally and from mainstream universities.

Course credits can be earned via examination, online study, and via the traditional correspondence format. Many of these programs allow you to simply register for whatever courses you wish to take without any entry formalities. Upon completion of the course you receive credits posted on an official transcript. In Appendix 3, we have reproduced some of the course credits by examination material from Ohio University, as an example. This method can also allow you to obtain transcript samples from a legitimate school for forgery purposes. Simply register for a correspondence course, and after you finish it, order a copy of your own transcript.

CHAPTER THIRTEEN

New Identity After 9/11 — What to Expect

The horrific events of September 11th have created new complications for those seeking to establish a new identity. It turned out that some of the terrorists had used fake identities or fake documentation to aid them in their criminal enterprise. Although the creation and use of fake ID was not a critical part of the nefarious plans that culminated in the destruction of the World Trade Center towers, fake ID did allow some parts of the terrorists' plans to proceed more easily and more efficiently. Right now, the states and the federal government are considering numerous proposals that will make it harder to obtain most types of identity documents. So the central questions to be considered are: What are these proposed changes, how likely are they to be implemented, and what would be a successful strategy for creating a new identity in this atmosphere of enhanced scrutiny?

In the United States, most identity documents are issued by the individual states. This panoply of identity documents includes such things as state identity cards, driver's licenses, birth certificates, fishing licenses, hunting licenses, and voter registration cards. Local municipalities issue things such as transit passes and library cards. Then there is an additional level of documentation issued by quasi-governmental entities, such as the student identity cards issued by colleges and universities. Private organizations also issue identity documents — health club membership passes, insurance identification cards, bank account ATM cards, etc.

Unlike in most other nations, the U.S. federal government does not issue the majority of identity documents carried by most people. The most common federal identification document is the Social Security card, the only federal identification most Americans will ever obtain. The federal government also issues passports, but only a small minority of Americans ever get a passport, because the foreign countries Americans visit most — Canada, Mexico and the Caribbean nations — do not require a passport for entry or return to the United States.

Driver's License

On a daily basis, the driver's license or state identity card are the fundamental identity documents used in America. When someone asks to see identification, they are in fact asking to see one of these documents. This has come about because most Americans learn how to drive a car, and most people in the United States depend upon a private automobile to get to work. Each state issues driver's licenses, and each state has its own requirements for issuance.

In general, most of these requirements include that the applicant be at least 16 years of age, be a resident of the state in question, establish proof of his or her identity, and not be under a license suspension or revocation in another jurisdiction. If these requirements are met, a written and driving test must be taken, fees paid, and the applicant will walk away with a new license, recognized from border to border.

Documents for Establishing Identity

To establish identity, the license applicant is required to provide a birth certificate — either an original or certified copy issued by the state, county, or municipal registrar. Additional secondary documentation must also be provided to establish the identity of the individual. What is acceptable will vary from state to state. Some states use a point system, where numerous different types of documents can be used, such as: health insurance cards, apartment leases, bank account ATM cards, etc. — so long as in the end, the applicant scores the required number of points under the system. In a few states, one can even obviate the need to show a birth certificate if enough of these documents are presented.

Some states require applicants to show explicit proof of their Social Security number during the licensing process. Most states will accept a variety of documents for this purpose: Social Security cards, payroll check stubs, even college transcripts that have the student's Social Security number on them. A few states require that the applicant show proof of residency in the state. This can be done by presenting a voter registration card, apartment lease or mortgage papers, or an insurance policy with a local address on it.

Once a person has obtained a driver's license or state identification card in one state, he can use it in any other state, and more importantly, easily exchange it for a different state's license or identity card. An exchange is faster and requires much less documentation than a new issue. The fact that the applicant already has a license or identity card from another state is proof in the new state that the person is who they say they are.

The Virginia Loophole

The September 11th terrorists exploited a loophole in the Virginia motor vehicle code to easily obtain driver's licenses in that state. In Virginia, you could arrange for a state resident to fill out a notarized affidavit attesting to the in-state residency of the license applicant. You then showed this affidavit to the motor vehicle clerk and she or he would process your application. Some of the suicide bombers had obtained Virginia licenses this way. Now all states are examining ways to make the issuance of driver's licenses more secure. Let's look at what some of these proposals are and how they would affect the public.

INS Documents

Many states are considering making the application procedure more complete, particularly in the case of non-U.S.-citizen applicants on temporary residence permits. These applicants carry identification documents issued by the Immigration and Naturalization Service. The problem the states face is that the validity of these documents cannot readily be determined. The INS issues plastic student visas and work permit identity cards to foreign nationals, and these cards look very much like driver's licenses. All states can verify online, in real time, an out-of-state license's validity, but they cannot do so with immigration documents. These documents can only be verified with INS, and that is a time-consuming and difficult process.

One proposal being considered is to make the database of all temporary residence visas and green cards verifiable at local motor vehicle department offices. This may happen in the future, but it is not being done right now because of the expense. Even if the funds are appropriated, it will take some time for this to be implemented. It is well known that immigration documents are hard to verify and many illegal immigrants successfully establish valid driver's licenses on the basis of these documents. High-quality forgeries of immigration documents are available for sale all across the country. The INS has responded by instituting tough new anti-counterfeiting features which make these documents harder to forge, but this has had an unintended effect. There are now numerous versions of the same document in circulation, all valid. By the time all of the previous versions have been superceded, the document fakers will have a flawless copy of the current-issue document ready for sale.

Some states have instituted new rules for foreigners here on temporary visas. Many states will now only issue a driver's license which is valid for one year, and some look different than those issued to American citizens. Other states have gone to mailing out the license to foreign applicants later, even if it is a state that normally has instant issuance of the final license. Clearly, one reality of September 11th is that foreign applicants from anywhere but Canada will face more scrutiny at motor vehicle departments, particularly people who are from Arab nations.

Social Security Numbers

The Social Security number requirement is receiving renewed attention. Some states require that the license applicant show proof of the Social Security number, but most do not verify the number presented with the Social Security Administration. Some states have outlawed the Social Security number requirement in driver licensing for privacy reasons. It has been proposed that all states require the Social Security number as part of the licensing process, and that all states verify this number directly with the Social Security Administration. Would this have made any difference in the case of the September 11th terrorists? All of the terrorists had valid Social Security numbers, which would have been verified with no trouble. Why? Because all of the terrorists were in the United States legally. As a result, they had the necessary paperwork from the INS to qualify for valid Social Security numbers. There is also an unintended consequence from enforcing the Social

Security number requirement, one that has more relevance for most of the public on a daily basis. We can use California as an example.

Drawbacks to Requiring a Social Security Number

Into the early 1990s, it was easy for anyone to obtain a valid California driver's license. All you had to do was present a birth certificate and a little other documentation, pass the tests, and you would be duly licensed. It did not matter what country the birth certificate was from or what your immigration status was, legal or illegal. This is no small consideration in a state with over 2.5 million illegal immigrant residents. However, California now requires that proof of the Social Security number be provided, and this number is verified before the final, permanent driver's license is mailed out from Sacramento. California also requires anyone born outside of the United States to provide documents from the INS to validate their "legal residence" within the United States.

The unintended consequence of these actions has been a rapid increase in the number of unlicensed, uninsured drivers on the roads in California. The fact is, illegal immigrants live in the state and they will drive, one way or the other. So the central question is: Do you want these people driving with valid licenses and auto insurance, or the current situation, where they have neither? Many people in California, who have been in accidents with these unlicensed, uninsured drivers, probably wish the law had not been changed.

Some states have seen the folly of this. Utah, Texas, and North Carolina eliminated the Social Security number requirement, because all three of these states have large illegal immigrant populations. These states want these people to be safe, licensed, and insured motorists, and the only way that this can happen is if they are able to obtain a valid driver's license. The question of whether they are in the country at all is an issue for the federal government.

Many states have also eliminated Social Security number requirements on licenses for privacy reasons. The crime of identity theft has grown exponentially over the last decade, helped in large part by many states displaying the Social Security number on the license, or in many instances, using the Social Security number as the license number. Some states, such as Washington, have outlawed this requirement, and others, such as Alabama, request the number, but it does not appear on the license and it is not verified.

Biometrics

The next change states are considering is the use of biometrics on licenses. Biometrics is the use of theoretically unique physical identifiers, such as fingerprints, on the license document. Many states — for instance, California and Hawaii — already take a thumbprint from license applicants. The utility of fingerprints on a license is primarily to make sure that a person who lost a license does not turn around and obtain another license in the same state under a different name. It is hard to see how fingerprints could be very effective in curbing identity fraud unless all states use them in the licensing process, and then it would only deter someone from getting a second license in the same state. However, many states have explicitly outlawed the use of biometrics because of privacy law implications and the fact that it smacks of police procedure to the public.

Balancing Security and Service

The problem motor vehicle department administrators face is balancing security considerations against the need to serve the public efficiently and without excessive intrusion. All but a very few of the people at a motor vehicle office are there to carry out legal activities. Even with the current system, the lines and wait times at many motor vehicle offices across the country are long and increasing. Consider what would happen if every birth certificate, Social Security card, and immigration document was subjected to verification. Instead of accepting a rent receipt or lease as proof of residency, the state could also mail a card to your address which you would have to bring with you on a return visit to pick up your final license. These cards would have to be individually numbered to guard against counterfeiting, and backed up with a database to verify them when presented. This would complicate the licensing process even more and cost the states much more money.

Possible Changes in Procedure

What changes are we likely to see? First, clerks will be given more training in how to spot fake documents. There will be a tightening of the requirements of what is acceptable documentation. Where before a notarized copy of something might have been accepted, now only certified copies or originals will do. Certainly, people from Middle Eastern countries will face much higher degrees of scrutiny, and the INS will institute new training for motor vehicle clerks on how to spot immigration-document forgeries. It is possible that a real-time verification system for immigration documents will be instituted. The licenses themselves will become harder to forge, with more holograms, multiple pictures, and other anti-counterfeiting features.

In light of this, is it still possible for a new-identity seeker to obtain a driver's license or state identity card in a new name? The answer is yes — with certain caveats. Anyone who has read my other books on new-identity creation understands that the key to a successful new identity is extensive preparation. First, some states are harder than other states. If the new identity seeker does not have a verifiable Social Security number, do not apply in a state that makes this a mandatory requirement and performs verifications. This information can be determined by going to the various state motor vehicle department web sites and carefully reading what the requirements are. You can also call the public service phone numbers of these agencies and ask what they require. One way to get extremely detailed information when you call is to say that you are an American returning from overseas after 15 years, and you need to know what to bring with you. This is an excellent strategy, because they will assume you have not had a license from any state before, and will have to provide the maximum amount of documentation.

Older first-time applicants — people past 30 — have always faced more scrutiny, but not because of terrorism. It is assumed if you are over 30, and do not have a license, you must have had one before, but it was suspended or revoked. The motor vehicle clerks check your name and birth through what is known as the National Driver Register (NDR). The NDR is a listing of everyone in the country whose licenses have been suspended or revoked. Motor vehicle clerks do this online while you are waiting.

Most motor vehicle clerks have been given training in how to spot forgeries of birth certificates. But this training is complicated by the simple fact that there are hundreds, if not thousands, of different types and styles of birth certificates in use. Birth certificates are issued by both county and state registrars in most states, and many larger cities still issue birth certificates. Birth certificates from the same office but from different years will look different. Seals will vary, and some states and counties also issue wallet-sized birth cards.

Motor vehicle clerks are taught to look for an embossed seal and signature, numbers that are typical for birth certificates from that jurisdiction, and to be suspicious if the person and the document do not seem to match. A good example would be someone who presents a birth certificate from West Virginia, but who is clearly Hispanic and speaks little or no English. Many of the books on new identity-creation explain in detail what real birth certificates look like and what information the new-identity seeker should make sure is on his birth document.

Be Prepared

Clerks are also trained to look at the entire picture presented. This is why it is crucial, particularly post-September 11, to be completely prepared. A person waltzing into a motor vehicle office with just a birth certificate is automatically suspect. The new-identity seeker should obtain as much documentation as possible before going to the motor vehicle department. If you are denied for some reason, you want it to be simply a matter of you did not have something they need, not because they are suspicious of you. The way to avoid suspicion is to go to their office with a wallet brimming full of secondary documents, obtained over time, along with your birth certificate.

This means obtaining a voter registration card, health insurance card, YMCA card, library card, transit pass, etc., before you go. An excellent source of photo identification is a student identification card issued by a local college or university. Register for one course and the card is yours. Frequently, you can get the ID as soon as you register, even if you have not paid your fees. Bank ATM/debit cards can be obtained by applying for a bank account online, and these are frequently accepted as secondary sources of identification. In the clerk's mind, someone with all of this detritus of life must be the real deal.

What must be avoided are mail-order birth certificates and other mass-produced identity documents. Post-September 11, the surveillance of these document sellers has been increased, and even if they sell their wares within the law, the government will compile samples of the goods and distribute copies of these documents to motor vehicle departments nationwide. Anyone using these documents will be detected and probably prosecuted. With computer technology, most people can produce birth certificates at home that are as good, or better, as those issued by the state.

So, we can conclude that the result of September 11th for fake ID is to create new hurdles, but none that are impassable. The new-identity seeker will just have to be more careful and meticulous in his preparation, and stay informed as to the best places to penetrate the system.

Recommended Reading

Acquiring New ID, by Ragnar Benson, Paladin Press.

Be Your Own Dick, Private Investigating Made Easy, Second Edition, by John Q. Newman, Loompanics Unlimited.

Bears' Guide to Earning Degrees by Distance Learning, 14th Edition, by John B. Bear and Mariah P. Bear, Ten Speed Press.

Bears' Guide to the Best Computer Degrees by Distance Learning, by John Bear, Mariah Bear, and Larry McQueary, Ten Speed Press.

Bears' Guide to the Best MBAs by Distance Learning, by John Bear and Mariah Bear, Ten Speed Press.

Birth Certificate Fraud, by U.S. Inspector General, Breakout Productions.

Counterfeit ID Made Easy, by Jack Luger, Loompanics Unlimited.

Credit Power!, by John Q. Newman, Breakout Productions.

Fake I.D. by Mail and Modem, by Trent Sands, Loompanics Unlimited.

Fraudulent Credentials, U.S. House of Representatives Report, Loompanics Unlimited.

Heavy Duty New Identity, Revised and Expanded Second Edition, by John Q. Newman, Breakout Productions.

How to Disappear Completely and Never Be Found, by Doug Richmond, Loompanics Unlimited.

The ID Forger, by John Q. Newman, Loompanics Unlimited.

Identity Theft: The Cybercrime of the Millennium, by John Q. Newman, Loompanics Unlimited.

The Modern Identity Changer, by Sheldon Charrett, Paladin Press.

New I.D. in America, by Anonymous, Paladin Press.

The Paper Trip III, by Barry Reid, Eden Press.

Reborn In Canada, Third Edition, by Trent Sands, Breakout Productions.

Reborn in the USA, Third Edition, by Trent Sands, Breakout Productions.

Understanding U.S. Identity Documents, by John Q. Newman, Breakout Productions.

Appendices

Appendix 1

NEVADA REVISED STATUTES
NRS 41.270
Proceedings to Change of Persons Names

3.223 JURISDICTION OF FAMILY COURTS
1. In each judicial district in which it is established, the family court has original, exclusive jurisdiction in any proceeding:
    (a) Brought pursuant to chapter 82, 123, 125, 125A, 125B, 126, 127, 128, 129, 130, 159, 425 or 432B of NRS.
    (b) Brought Pursuant to chapter 31A of NRS, except to the extent that NRS 31A.010 authorizes the use of any other judicial or administrative procedure to facilitate the collection of an obligation for support.
    (c) Brought Pursuant to NRS 442.255 and 442.2555 to request the court to issue an order authorizes an abortion.
    (d) For judicial approval of the marriage of a minor.
    (e) Otherwise within the jurisdiction of the juvenile court.
    (f) To establish the date of birth, place of birth or parentage of a minor.
    (g) To change the name of a minor.
    (h) For a judicial declaration of the sanity of a minor.
    (i) To approve the withholding or withdrawal of life-sustaining procedures from a person as authorized by law.
    (j) Brought pursuant to NRS 433A.200 to 433A.330, inclusive, for an involuntary court-ordered admission to a mental health facility.
2. The family court, where established, and the justices' court have concurrent jurisdiction over actions for the issuance of a temporary or extended order for protection against domestic violence.

41.230 ACTIONS CONCERNING PERSONS

    41.230 Hearing.
    Upon the hearing of the petition the court may require information appearing to be pertinent to the particular case at hand, and the court may require the presence of any person, or the affidavit of such person if he is out of the jurisdiction of the court, as to enable the court to be fully advised in the premises.

    41.240 Court order establishing facts as presented to court.
    After the court deems the evidence presented upon the hearing of the petition sufficient to grant the prayer of the petitioner, it shall make an order establishing the facts of the mailer as presented to the court.

    41.250 Verified Petition;
    Any person desiring to have their name changed may file a verified petition with the clerk of the district court of the district in which they reside. The petition shall be added to the court and shall state the applicant's present name, the name which they desire to bear in the future, the reason for desiring the change of name and whether they have been convicted of a felony.

    41.250 Filing of decree.
    Any decree rendered under the provisions of NRS 41.210 to 11.260, inclusive, shall be filed with the state health officer and in the office of the county recorder of the county in which the decree is rendered.

PROCEEDINGS TO CHANGE NAMES OF PERSONS

41270 Verified petition.

Any person desiring to have his name changed may file a verified petition with the clerk of the district court of the district in which he resides. The petition shall be addressed to the court and shall state the applicant's present name, the name which he desires to bear in the future, the reason for desiring the change and whether he has been convicted of a felony.

41.280 Publication of notice.

Upon the filing of the petition the applicant shall make out and procure a notice, which shall state the fact of the filing of the petition, its object, his present name and the name which he desires to bear in the future. The notice shall be published in some newspaper of general circulation, in the county once a week for 3 successive weeks.

41.290 Order of court; hearing on objections; disposition and recession of order.

1. If, within 10 days after the last publication of the notice no written objection is filed with the clerk, upon proof of the filing of the petition and publication of notice as required in NRS 41.280, and upon being satisfied by the statements of the petition, or by other evidence, that good reason exists therefore, the court shall make an order changing the name of the applicant and shall appoint a day for hearing the proofs, respectively, of the applicant and the objection, upon reasonable notice. Upon that day the court shall hear the proofs, and grant or refuse the prayer of the petitioner according to whether the proofs show satisfactory reasons for making the change.

2. Upon the making of an order either granting or denying the prayer of the applicant, the order must be recorded as a judgment of the court. If the petition is granted, the name of the applicant must there upon be as stated in the order and the clerk shall transmit a certified copy of the order to the state register of vital statistics.

3. If an order grants a change of name to a person who has a record, the clerk shall transmit a certified copy of the order to the central repository for Nevada records for criminal history for inclusion in the person's record of criminal history.

4. Upon receiving uncontrovertible proof that an applicant in their petition falsely denied having been convicted of a felony, the court shall rescind its order granting the change of name and the clerk shall transmit a certified copy of the order rescinding the previous order to:
    (a) The state registrar of vital statistics for inclusion in their records:
    (b) The central repository of Nevada records of criminal history for inclusion in their record of criminal history.

VITAL STATISTICS

440.310 Vital Statistics

1. Application for a birth certificate pursuant to this section must be made in writing on a form supplied by the state registrar and be accompanied by:
    (a) The document for which a replacement is sought.
    (b) A translation of the document.
    (c) An affidavit executed by the translator before a person who is authorized to administer oaths, attesting to the accuracy of the translation.
    (d) A certificate from the United States Immigration and Naturalization Service which establishes that the person who is the subject of the document has entered the United States legally.
    (e) The fee required by this chapter for the making and certification of the record of any birth by the state registrar.

2. When he receives an application and the documents required by this section, the state registrar shall prepare a birth certificate and clearly mark it on its face:

"ISSUED TO REPLACE A BIRTH RECORD FROM _____ IN THE _____ LANGUAGE."

440.305 Certificate of birth:
State registrar to change the name on certificate upon request of certain persons. Upon request of a person or his parent, guardian, or legal representative, and after receipt of a certified copy of an order of the court changing the name of such person, whether such order was entered prior or subsequent to July 1, 1980, the state registrar shall indicate the change of name on the certificate of birth of such person.

440.310 Adopted children:
Supplementary certificate; report of adoption, amendment or annulment of order or decree of adoption; availability of records on court order.
1. Whenever the state registrar receives a certified report of adoption, amendment or annulment of adoption filed in accordance with the provisions of NRS 127.157 or the laws of another state or foreign country or a codified copy of the adoption decree he shall prepare a supplementary certificate of birth in the new name of the adopted person which; shows the adoptive parents as the parents, and, except as provided in subsection 2, seal and file the report or decree and the original certificate of birth.
2. Whenever the state registrar receives a certified report of adoption, amendment or annulment of an order or decree of adoption from a court concerning a person born outside this state, the report must be forwarded to the office responsible for vital statistics in the person's state of birth, if the birth occurred in a foreign country, the report must be returned to the attorney or agency handling the adoption for submission to the appropriate federal agency unless a birth certificate has been prepared pursuant to NRS 440.303, in which case the state registrar shall, if he receives evidence that:
    (a) The person being adopted is a citizen of the United States and;
    (b) The adoptive parents are residents of Nevada, prepare a supplementary certificate of birth as described in subsection 1.
3. Sealed documents may be opened only upon an order of the court issuing the adoption decree, expressly so permitting, pursuant to a petition setting forth the reasons therefor.

NOTE: Each District Court has it's own rules and regulations as to the paper used and Court styling. Check with your local District Clerk and they will give you a copy of the rules. Below is outlined for Clark County and most of the other Districts. Courts will change from time to time as to the requirements.

NOTE: In the Eighth District Court there has been some recent changes:
1. The documents shall have a two-hole punch at the top and in the center of the documents.
2. The word ORIGINAL shall be stapled in large (20 point) letters between the two holes.
3. At the top of the documents, before the name of the petitioner, shall be the code for the action. Name change code PCON (this means Petitioner Change of Name)

EIGHTH DISTRICT COURT RULE 7.20: FORM OF PAPERS PRESENTED FOR FILING; EXHIBITS' DOCUMENTS; LEGAL CITATIONS.

(a) All pleading's and papers presented for filing must be flat, unfolded, firmly bounded together at the top, on white paper of standard quality, not less than 16-lb. weight and 8½ X 11 inches in size. All papers must be typewritten or prepared by some other duplication process that will produce clear and permanent copies equally legible to printing. All print shall be of a size providing no more than 10 characters per linear inch; e.g. pica. Carbon or photocopies may not be filed, except as provided in paragraphs (d) and (f) of this rule. Only one side of the paper must be used. The lines of each page must be double-spaced, except that descriptions of real property may be single-spaced. All quotations of more than 50 words must be indented and single-spaced. Pages must be numbered consecutively at the bottom. Lines of pages must be numbered in the left hand margin.

(b) No original pleading or paper may be amended by making erasures or interlineation thereon, or by attaching slips thereto, expect by leave of court.

(c) The following information shall be stated upon the first page of every paper presented for filing, single-spaced. (1) The name, Nevada State Bar identification number, address and telephone number of the attorney and any associated attorney appearing for the party filing the paper and whether such attorney appears for the plaintiff, defendant, or other party, or the name, address, and telephone number of a party appearing in person, shall be set forth in the space to the left of the center of the page beginning at the top of the first page. The space to the right of center shall be reserved for the filing marks of the clerk.

(d) The title of the court which is designated as District Court Clark County, or other county, shall appear at the center of the first page at least one inch below the information required by paragraph (1).

DISTRICT COURT
CLARK COUNTY, NEVADA

(3) Below the title of the court, there shall be inserted in the space to the left of center of the paper the name of the action or proceeding, i.e.;

```
JOHN DOE,              )
        Plaintiff,     )
-vs-                   )
                       )
RICHARD ROE            )
        Defendant,     )
```

(4) In the space to the right of center, there shall be inserted this case number, the department number, and the docket number as follows:

CASE NO.
DEPT. NO.
DOCKET NO.

(5) The title of the pleading, motion or other document, sufficient in description to appraise the respondent and clerk of the nature of the document filed, or the relief sought, e.g.: Plaintiff's Motion to Compel Answers to Interrogatories; Defendant's Motion for Summary Judgment against John Doe, Plaintiff John Doe's Interrogatories to Defendant Roe; Order Granting Plaintiff Doe's Motion for Summary Judgment against Defendant Roe, must be typed or printed to the right of center under the Docket number or to be centered on this page directly below the name of the parties to the action or proceeding.

90

For the convenience of the court and the parties, the same title used on the motion papers must appear on all calendars at the time of the hearing.

(SAMPLE)
DISTRICT COURT
CLARK COUNTY, NEVADA

JOHN DOE	)		
Plaintiff,	)		
-vs-	)	CASE NO.	
RICHARD ROE,	)	DEPT NO.	
Defendant,	)	DOCKET NO.	

MOTION, ORDER, REPLY, JUDGMENT, ETC.

Date of Hearing:
Time of Hearing:

(6) If the paper to be filed is a response, reply or other document related matter which has already been set for hearing but not yet heard, the time and date of the hearing shall appear immediately below the title of the paper.

    (d) All exhibits attached to the pleading or papers must be in 8½ x 11 inches in size. Exhibits which are smaller must be affixed to a blank sheet of paper of the appropriate size. Exhibits which are larger than 8½ x 11 inches in size must be reduced to 8½ x 11 or must be folded as to measure 8½ x 11 inches in size. All exhibits attached to pleading or papers must clearly show the exhibit number at the bottom or on the right side thereof. Plaintiffs must use numerical designations and defendants must use alphabetical designations. Copies of exhibits must be clearly legible and not unnecessarily voluminous. Original documents must be retained by counsel for introduction as exhibits at the time of a hearing or at the time of trial rather than attached to pleading.

(7) With the exception of printed forms furnished by the Country Clerk's Office, a list of which may usually be obtained at the Clerk's Office, all pleading's and documents filed MUST BE:

    (a) On legal cap, of good quality and without interlineations except by leave of court.

    (b) Original typewritten pages, using one side of the paper only, double-spaced and numbered consecutively at the center bottom of the page. Real estate descriptions may be single-spaced and all quotations of more than 50 words must be indented and single-spaced.

    (c) If copies of documents instead of originals must be submitted, they MUST be retyped or consistent of a copying process which is clearly legible.

LOCAL RULES of DISTRICT COURT

Keep informed of the local District Court Rules for your District
Eighth Judicial District Court Rule 7:23

Social Security Administration Application for a Social Security Card

SOCIAL SECURITY ADMINISTRATION Application for a Social Security Card

Form Approved
OMB No. 0960-0066

1	**NAME** TO BE SHOWN ON CARD →	First	Full Middle Name	Last

FULL NAME AT BIRTH IF OTHER THAN ABOVE → First   Full Middle Name   Last

OTHER NAMES USED →

2 **MAILING ADDRESS** → Do Not Abbreviate
Street Address, Apt. No., PO Box, Rural Route No
City   State   Zip Code

3 **CITIZENSHIP** (Check One) →
☐ U.S. Citizen ☐ Legal Alien Allowed To Work ☐ Legal Alien **Not Allowed** To Work ☐ Other (See Instructions On Page 1)

4 **SEX** → ☐ Male ☐ Female

5 **RACE/ETHNIC DESCRIPTION** (Check One Only—Voluntary) →
☐ Asian Asian-American or Pacific Islander ☐ Hispanic ☐ Black (Not Hispanic) ☐ North American Indian or Alaskan Native ☐ White (Not Hispanic)

6 **DATE OF BIRTH** Month, Day, Year   **7** **PLACE OF BIRTH** (Do Not Abbreviate)   City   State or Foreign Country   FCI   Office Use Only

8 **A. MOTHER'S MAIDEN NAME** → First   Full Middle Name   Last Name At Her Birth

B. MOTHER'S SOCIAL SECURITY NUMBER (Complete only if applying for a number for a child under age 18.) → ☐☐☐ – ☐☐ – ☐☐☐☐

9 **A. FATHER'S NAME** → First   Full Middle Name   Last

B. FATHER'S SOCIAL SECURITY NUMBER (Complete only if applying for a number for a child under age 18.) → ☐☐☐ – ☐☐ – ☐☐☐☐

10 Has the applicant or anyone acting on his/her behalf ever filed for or received a Social Security number card before?
☐ Yes (If "yes", answer questions 11-13.) ☐ No (If "no", go on to question 14.) ☐ Don't Know (If "don't know", go on to question 14.)

11 Enter the Social Security number previously assigned to the person listed in item 1. → ☐☐☐ – ☐☐ – ☐☐☐☐

12 Enter the name shown on the most recent Social Security card issued for the person listed in item 1. → First   Middle   Last

13 Enter any different date of birth if used on an earlier application for a card. → Month, Day, Year

14 **TODAY'S DATE** Month, Day, Year   **15** **DAYTIME PHONE NUMBER** ( ) Area Code   Number

DELIBERATELY FURNISHING (OR CAUSING TO BE FURNISHED) FALSE INFORMATION ON THIS APPLICATION IS A CRIME PUNISHABLE BY FINE OR IMPRISONMENT, OR BOTH.

16 **YOUR SIGNATURE** ▶   **17** **YOUR RELATIONSHIP TO THE PERSON IN ITEM 1 IS:**
☐ Self ☐ Natural or Adoptive Parent ☐ Legal Guardian ☐ Other (Specify)

DO NOT WRITE BELOW THIS LINE (FOR SSA USE ONLY)					
NPN			DOC	NTI	CAN	ITV
PBC	EVI	EVA	EVC	PRA	NWR	DNR	UNIT

EVIDENCE SUBMITTED

SIGNATURE AND TITLE OF EMPLOYEE(S) REVIEWING EVIDENCE AND/OR CONDUCTING INTERVIEW

DATE

DCL   DATE

92

WHEN YOU APPLY FOR A CHILD'S
SOCIAL SECURITY NUMBER

You may need this additional information to complete items 8.B and 9.B. on Form SS-5, Application for a Social Security Card.

When you apply for a Social Security number for a child under age 18, you need to provide each parent's Social Security number **unless** the –
* parent does not have a Social Security number;
* parent's Social Security number is not known.

If you can't provide the parent's Social Security number for one of the reasons listed above, we'll still be able to assign the child a Social Security number.

∧∧∧

CUANDO USTED SOLICTIA UN NÚMERO
DE SEGURO SOCIAL PARA UN NIÑO

Usted podría necesitar esta información adicional para completar los articulos 8.B y 9.B. en el formulario SS-5, *Solicitud para una tarjeta de Seguro Social.*

Cuando usted solicita números de Seguro Social para un niño menor de 18 años, necesita proveer los números de Seguro Social de cada padre **a menos que** –
* los padres no tengan números de Seguro Social;
* los números de Seguro Social de los padres sean desconocidos.

Si usted no puede proveer los números de Seguro Social de los padres por una de las razones mencionadas arriba, todavía podremos asignar un número de Seguro Social al niño(a).

Form **SS-5-SUP** (05-2000)

SOCIAL SECURITY ADMINISTRATION
Application for a Social Security Card

Applying for a Social Security Card is easy AND it is FREE!

If you DO NOT follow these instructions, we CANNOT process your application!

STEP 1 Complete and sign the application with BLUE or BLACK ink. Do NOT use pencil! Follow instructions below.

STEP 2 See Page 2 to determine what evidence we need.

STEP 3 Submit the application and evidence to any Social Security office. Follow instructions below.

HOW TO COMPLETE THE APPLICATION

Most items on the form are self-explanatory. Those that need explanation are discussed below. The numbers match the numbered items on the form. If you are completing this form for someone else, please complete the items as they apply to that person.

2. Show an address where you can receive the card 10 to 14 days from now.

3. If you check "other" for CITIZENSHIP, provide a document from the Federal/State or local agency explaining why you need a Social Security number and that you meet all the requirements for the benefit or service except for a number.

5. You do not have to complete this item about race/ethnic background. We use this information for statistical reports on how Social Security programs affect people. We do not reveal the identities of individuals.

6. Show the month, day, and full (4-digit) year of birth, for example, "1998" for year of birth.

8. You **must** enter the mother's Social Security number in item 8B. if you are applying for a number for a child under age 18.

9. You **must** enter the father's Social Security number in item 9B. if you are applying for a number for a child under age 18.

13. If the date of birth you show in item 6 is different from the date of birth you used on a prior application for a Social Security number card, show the date of birth you used on the prior application and submit evidence of age to support the date of birth in item 6.

16. You **must** sign the application if you are age 18 or older and are physically and mentally capable. If you are under age 18, you may also sign the application if you are physically and mentally capable. If you cannot sign your name, you should sign with an "X" mark and have two people sign as witnesses in the space beside the mark. If you are physically or mentally incapable, generally a parent, close relative, or legal guardian may sign the application. Call us if you need clarification about who can sign.

HOW TO SUBMIT THE APPLICATION

Mail the form and your evidence documents to the nearest Social Security office. We will return your documents to you. If you do not want to mail your original documents, take them to the nearest Social Security office with this application.

If you are age 18 or older and have never been assigned a number before, you must apply in person.

EVIDENCE WE NEED

CAUTION: We cannot accept photocopies of documents. You must submit original documents or copies certified by the custodian of the record. **Notarized copies are not acceptable.** If your documents do not meet this requirement, we cannot process your application. We will return your documents. IF YOU DO NOT WANT TO MAIL YOUR ORIGINAL DOCUMENTS, TAKE THEM TO ANY SOCIAL SECURITY OFFICE.

If you need an **ORIGINAL CARD** (you have NEVER been assigned a Social Security number before), you must show us proof of :

> **AGE,**
> **IDENTITY, and**
> **U.S. CITIZENSHIP or LAWFUL ALIEN STATUS**

If you need a **DUPLICATE CARD** (no name change), you must show us proof of **IDENTITY**.

IMPORTANT: If you were born outside the U.S., you must also show us proof of
U.S. CITIZENSHIP or LAWFUL ALIEN STATUS.

If you need a **CORRECTED CARD** because of a name change, you must show us proof of **IDENTITY**.

To **CHANGE YOUR NAME** on our records, we need one or more documents identifying you by your OLD NAME on our records and your NEW NAME.

IMPORTANT: If you were born outside the U.S., you must also show us proof of
U.S. CITIZENSHIP or LAWFUL ALIEN STATUS.

AGE: We prefer to see your birth certificate. However, we can accept other documents such as a hospital record of your birth made before you were age 5 or a religious record made before you were three months old. If you were born outside the U.S., we can accept your passport. Call us for advice if you cannot obtain any of these documents.

IDENTITY: We must see a document in the name you want shown on the card. We can generally accept a current document that has enough information to identify you (e.g., signature, name, age, date of birth, parents' names). **We CANNOT ACCEPT a BIRTH CERTIFICATE, HOSPITAL BIRTH RECORD, SSN CARD, SSN CARD STUB, OR SSA RECORD.** Some documents that we can accept are:

- Driver's license
- Employer ID card
- Passport

- Marriage or divorce record
- Adoption record
- Health Insurance card (not a Medicare card)

- Military records
- Insurance policy
- School ID card

IMPORTANT: If you are applying for a card on behalf of someone else, we must see proof of identity for both you and the person to whom the card will be issued.

NAME CHANGE: If your name is now different from the name shown on your card, we need an identity document that identifies you by BOTH your old name AND your new name. Examples include a marriage certificate, divorce decree, or a court order that changes your name. Or we can accept two identity documents—one in your old name and one in your new name. (See IDENTITY for examples of identity documents.)

U.S. CITIZENSHIP: We can accept most documents that show you were born in the U.S. If you are a U.S. citizen born outside the U.S., show us a U.S. consular report of birth, a U.S. passport, a Certificate of Citizenship, or a Certificate of Naturalization.

ALIEN STATUS: We need to see a current document issued to you by the U.S. Immigration and Naturalization Service (INS), such as Form I-551, I-94, I-688B, or I-766. We CANNOT accept a receipt showing you applied for the document. If you are not authorized to work in the U.S., we can issue you a Social Security card if you are lawfully here and need the number for a valid nonwork reason. Your card will be marked to show you cannot work, and, if you do, we will notify INS.

IF YOU HAVE ANY QUESTIONS: If you have any questions about this form, or about the documents you need to show us, please contact any Social Security office. A telephone call will help you make sure you have everything you need to apply for a card.

THE PAPERWORK/PRIVACY ACT AND YOUR APPLICATION

The Privacy Act of 1974 requires us to give each person the following notice when applying for a Social Security number.

Sections 205(c) and 702 of the Social Security Act allow us to collect the facts we ask for on this form.

We use the facts you provide on this form to assign you a Social Security number and to issue you a Social Security card. You do not have to give us these facts, however, without them we cannot issue you a Social Security number or a card. Without a number, you may not be able to get a job and could lose Social Security benefits in the future.

The Social Security number is also used by the Internal Revenue Service for tax administration purposes as an identifier in processing tax returns of persons who have income which is reported to the Internal Revenue Service and by persons who are claimed as dependents on someone's Federal income tax return.

We may disclose information as necessary to administer Social Security programs, including to appropriate law enforcement agencies to investigate alleged violations of Social Security law; to other government agencies for administering entitlement, health, and welfare programs such as Medicaid, Medicare, veterans benefits, military pension, and civil service annuities, black lung, housing, student loans, railroad retirement benefits, and food stamps; to the Internal Revenue Service for Federal tax administration; and to employers and former employers to properly prepare wage reports. We may also disclose information as required by Federal law, for example, to the Department of Justice, Immigration and Naturalization Service, to identify and locate aliens in the U.S.; to the Selective Service System for draft registration; and to the Department of Health and

Human Services for child support enforcement purposes. We may verify Social Security numbers for State motor vehicle agencies that use the number in issuing drivers licenses, as authorized by the Social Security Act. Finally, we may disclose information to your Congressional representative if they request information to answer questions you ask him or her.

We may use the information you give us when we match records by computer. Matching programs compare our records with those of other Federal, State, or local government agencies to determine whether a person qualifies for benefits paid by the Federal government. The law allows us to do this even if you do not agree to it.

Explanations about these and other reasons why information you provide us may be used or given out are available in Social Security offices. If you want to learn more about this, contact any Social Security office.

The Paperwork Reduction Act of 1995 requires us to notify you that this information collection is in accordance with the clearance requirements of section 3507 of the Paperwork Reduction Act of 1995. We may not conduct or sponsor, and you are not required to respond to, a collection of information unless it displays a valid OMB control number.

TIME IT TAKES TO COMPLETE THIS FORM

We estimate that it will take you about 8.5 to 9 minutes to provide the information. This includes the time it will take to read the instructions, gather the necessary facts and provide the information. All requests for Social Security cards and other claims-related information **should be sent to your local Social Security office**, whose address is listed under Social Security Administration in the U.S. Government section of your telephone directory. Comments or suggestions on our "Time it Takes" estimate are welcome and should be addressed to: Social Security Administration, ATTN: Reports Clearance Officer, 1-A-21 Operations Building, Baltimore, MD 21235-0001. SEND ONLY COMMENTS ON OUR "TIME IT TAKES" ESTIMATE TO THIS ADDRESS.

Identity Theft
Complaint Input Form

If you believe you have been the victim of identity theft, you may use the form below to send a complaint to the Federal Trade Commission (FTC). The information you provide is up to you. However, if you don't provide your name and other information, it may be impossible for us to refer, respond to, or investigate your complaint or request. To learn how we use the information you provide, please read our <u>Privacy Policy</u> (https://rn.ftc.gov/dod).

The FTC serves as the federal clearinghouse for complaints by victims of identity theft. While the FTC does not resolve individual consumer problems, your complaint helps us investigate fraud, and can lead to law enforcement action. The FTC enters Internet, telemarketing, identity theft and other fraud-related complaints into *Consumer Sentinel*, a secure, online database available to hundreds of civil and criminal law enforcement agencies worldwide.

We use secure socket layer (SSL) encryption to protect the transmission of the information you submit. The information you provide is stored securely offline.

If you want to file a complaint with the FTC about a problem other than identity theft, please use the Federal Trade Commission online <u>complaint form</u>.

How Do We Reach You?

First Name: _____

Last Name: _____

Street Address: _____

Apt. or Suite No.: _____

City: _____

State/Province: _____

Zip: _____-_____

Country: _____

Home Phone: _____ _____   **Work Phone:** _____ _____ **Ext.** _____
          (Area Code) (Phone Number)   *(Area Code) (Phone Number)*   *(Extension)*

Social Security _____-_____-_____   **Date of Birth:** _____(MM/DD/YY)
Number: *(Numbers Only)*   *(Numbers Only)*

Email Address: _____(i.e., anyone@myisp.com)

98

Tell Us About Your Problem

1. Types of Identity Theft You Have Experienced.

ID Theft occurs when someone uses your name or other identifying information for their personal gain. Please check the types of ID theft you were a victim of. (Check as many as apply).

- ❑ **Credit Cards**
- ❑ **Checking or Savings Accounts**
- ❑ **Loans**
- ❑ **Phone or Utilities**

- ❑ **Securities or Other Investments**
- ❑ **Internet or E-Mail**
- ❑ **Government Documents or Benefits**
- ❑ **Other**

Did suspect use the Internet to open the account or purchase goods or services?

- ❑ Yes
- ❑ No
- ❑ Don't Know

2. Describe Your Complaint Here.

Please give us information about the identity theft, including, but not limited to, how the theft occurred, who may be responsible for the theft, and what actions you have taken since the theft. Please include a list of companies where fraudulent accounts were established or your current accounts were affected. Please limit your complaint to 2000 characters.

| |
| |
| |
| |
| |

3. Details of the Identity Theft.

When did you notice you might be a victim of identity theft? _____
(MM/DD/YYYY)

When did the identity theft first occur? (i.e., when was the first account opened?):_____
(MM/DD/YYYY)

How many accounts (credit cards, loans, bank accounts, cellular phone accounts, etc.) were opened or accessed? _____

How much money, if any, have you had to pay? _____
(Numbers Only)

How much money, if any, did the identity thief obtain from companies in your name? _____
(Numbers Only)

What other problems, if any, have you experienced as a result of the identity theft? (Examples: No nonmonetary damage; civil suit filed or judgment entered against you; criminal investigation, arrest or conviction; denied credit or other financial services; denied employment or loss of job; etc.)

4. The Identity Thief.

Please provide any information you may have about the identity thief, including his or her name, and any addresses or phone numbers the identity thief may have used.

First Name: _____

Last Name: _____

Street Address: _____

Apt. or Suite No.: _____

City: _____

State/Province: _____

Zip Code: _____ - _____

Country: _____

Phone Number: _____ - _____
                (Area Code) (Phone Number)
                (Numbers Only)

E-mail Address: _____
                (i.e., anyone@myisp.com)

Your relationship to the identity thief: _____

5. Contacts.

Please indicate which of the following steps, if any, you have already taken to deal with the identity theft. For which of the following credit bureaus, have you: (check all that apply)

Called to report the fraud?	❑ Equifax	❑ Experian	❑ Trans Union ❑ Other	❑ None
Put a "fraud alert" on your report?	❑ Equifax	❑ Experian	❑ Trans Union ❑ Other	❑ None
Ordered your credit report?	❑ Equifax	❑ Experian	❑ Trans Union ❑ Other	❑ None
Problem with Credit Bureau?	❑ Equifax	❑ Experian	❑ Trans Union ❑ Other	❑ None
Have you contacted the police?	❑ Yes	❑ No		

100

If yes, please provide police department name? _____

Department State? _____

Report Number? ❑ Yes   ❑ No

If yes, please provide report number: _____

6. Problems With Companies.

Do you have any problems with the companies, credit bureaus, or organizations you are dealing with concerning your identity theft problems? If so, identify each company, credit bureau, or organization, provide its location and/or telephone number, if you have it, and tell us briefly what the problem is. **NOTE: If you checked the problem box for any of the three credit bureaus in the section above, please include those credit bureaus here.**

Company 1

Company Name: _____

City: _____

State/Province: _____

Zip Code: _____-_____

Country: _____

Phone Number: _____ _____ **Ext.** _____
        (Area Code)(Phone Number)   *(Extension) (Numbers Only)*

Have you notified this company? ❑ Yes   ❑ No

Have you sent written notifications to this company? ❑ Yes ❑ No

Company 2

Company Name: _____

City: _____

State/Province: _____

Zip Code: _____-_____

Country: _____

Phone Number: _____ _____ **Ext.** _____
        (Area Code)(Phone Number)   *(Extension) (Numbers Only)*

Have you notified this company? ❑ Yes   ❑ No

Have you sent written notifications to this company? ❑ Yes ❑ No

Company 3

Company Name: _____

City: _____

State/Province: _____

Zip Code: _____-_____

Country: _____

Phone Number: _____ _____ **Ext.** _____
        (Area Code)(Phone Number)   *(Extension) (Numbers Only)*

Have you notified this company? ❑ Yes   ❑ No

Have you sent written notifications to this company? ❑ Yes   ❑ No

ID Theft Affidavit

Victim Information

(1) My full legal name is _____
                 (First)   (Middle)   (Last)   (Jr., Sr., III)

(2) (If different from above) When the events described in this affidavit took place, I was known

as _____
        (First)   (Middle)   (Last)   (Jr., Sr., III)

(3) My date of birth is _____
                  (day/month/year)

(4) My social security number is _____.

(5) My driver's license or identification card state and number are _____

(6) My current address is _____

    City _____ State _____ Zip Code_____

(7) I have lived at this address since _____.
                            (month/year)

(8) (If different from above) When the events described in this affidavit took place, my address

was _____City _____State _____ Zip Code _____

(9) I lived at the address in #8 from _____ until _____.
                                 (month/year)   (month/year)

(10) My daytime telephone number is (___)_____

     My evening telephone number is (___)_____

How the Fraud Occurred

Check all that apply for items 11-17:

(11) ☐ I did not authorize anyone to use my name or personal information to seek the money, credit, loan, goods or services described in this report.

(12) ☐ I did not receive any benefit, money, goods or services as a result of the events described in this report.

(13) ☐ My identification documents (for example, credit cards; birth certificate; driver's license; social security card; etc.) were ☐ stolen ☐ lost on or about _____.
                                                   (day/month/year)

(14) ☐ To the best of my knowledge and belief, the following person(s) used my information (for example, my name, address, date of birth, existing account numbers, social security number, mother's maiden name, etc.) or identification documents to get money, credit, loans, goods or services without my knowledge or authorization:

_____	_____
Name (if known)	Name (if known)
_____	_____
Address (if known)	Address (if known)
_____	_____
Phone number(s) (if known)	Phone number(s) (if known)
_____	_____
Additional information (if known)	Additional information (if known)
_____	_____

(15) ☐ I do NOT know who used my information or identification documents to get money, credit, loans, goods or services without my knowledge or authorization.

(16) ☐ Additional comments: (For example, description of the fraud, which documents or information were used or how the identity thief gained access to your information.)

(Attach additional pages as necessary.)

Victim's Law Enforcement Actions

(17) (check one) I ☐ am ☐ am not willing to assist in the prosecution of the person(s) who committed this fraud.

(18) (check one) I ☐ am ☐ am not authorizing the release of this information to law enforcement for the purpose of assisting them in the investigation or prosecution of the person(s) who committed this fraud.

(19) (check all that apply) I ☐ have ☐ have not reported the events described in this affidavit to the police or other law enforcement agency. The police ☐ did ☐ did not write a report.

104

In the event you have contacted the police or other law enforcement agency, please complete the following:

Agency (#1)	(Officer/Agency personnel taking report)
(Date of report)	(Report Number, if any)
(Phone number)	(e-mail address, if any)
Agency (#2)	(Officer/Agency personnel taking report)
(Date of report)	(Report Number, if any)
(Phone number)	(e-mail address, if any)

Documentation Checklist

Please indicate the supporting documentation you are able to provide to the companies you plan to notify. Attach copies (NOT originals) to the affidavit before sending it to the companies.

(20) ☐ A copy of a valid government-issued photo-identification card (for example, your driver's license, state-issued ID card or your passport). If you are under 16 and don't have a photo-ID, you may submit a copy of your birth certificate or a copy of your official school records showing your enrollment and place of residence.

(21) ☐ Proof of residency during the time the disputed bill occurred, the loan was made or the other event took place (for example, a rental/lease agreement in your name, a copy of a utility bill or a copy of an insurance bill).

(22) ☐ A copy of the report you filed with the police or sheriff's department. If you are unable to obtain a report or report number from the police, please indicate that in Item 19. Some companies only need the report number, not a copy of the report. You may want to check with each company.

Signature

I declare under penalty of perjury that the information I have provided in this affidavit is true and correct to the best of my knowledge.

_____   _____
(signature)   (date signed)

Knowingly submitting false information on this form could subject you to criminal prosecution for perjury.

_____
(Notary)

[Check with each company. Creditors sometimes require notarization. If they do not, please have one witness (non-relative) sign below that you completed and signed this affidavit.]

Witness:

_____   _____
(signature)   (printed name)

_____   _____
(date)   (telephone number)

FRAUDULENT ACCOUNT STATEMENT

Completing this Statement

- Make as many copies of this page as you need. **Complete a separate page for each company you are notifying and only send it to that company.** Include a copy of your signed affidavit.

- List only the account(s) you're disputing with the company receiving this form. **See the example below**.

- If a collection agency sent you a statement, letter or notice about the fraudulent account, attach a copy of that document (**NOT** the original).

I declare (check all that apply):

☐ As a result of the event(s) described in the ID Theft Affidavit, the following account(s) was/were opened at your company in my name without my knowledge, permission or authorization using my personal information or identifying documents:

Creditor Name/Address (the company that opened the account or provided the goods or services)	Account Number	Type of unauthorized credit/goods/services provided by creditor (if known)	Date issued or opened (if known)	Amount/Value provided (the amount charged or the cost of the goods/services)
Example Example National Bank 22 Main Street Columbus, Ohio 22722	01234567-89	Auto loan	01/05/2000	$25,500.00

☐ During the time of the accounts described above, I had the following account open with your company:

Billing name _____

Billing address _____

Account number _____

Instructions for Completing the ID Theft Affidavit

To make certain that you do not become responsible for the debts incurred by the identity thief, you must provide proof that you didn't create the debt to each of the companies where accounts were opened or used in your name.

A working group composed of credit grantors, consumer advocates and the Federal Trade Commission (FTC) developed this ID Theft Affidavit to help you report information to many companies using just one standard form. Use of this affidavit is optional. While many companies accept this affidavit, others require that you submit more or different forms. Before you send the affidavit, contact each company to find out if they accept it.

You can use this affidavit where a **new account** was opened in your name. The information will enable the companies to investigate the fraud and decide the outcome of your claim. (If someone made unauthorized charges to an **existing account**, call the company to find out what to do.)

This affidavit has two parts:

*   **ID Theft Affidavit** is where you report general information about yourself and the theft.

*   **Fraudulent Account Statement** is where you describe the fraudulent account(s) opened in your name. Use a separate Fraudulent Account Statement for each company you need to write to.

When you send the affidavit to the companies, attach copies (**NOT** originals) of any supporting documents (e.g., driver's license, police report) you have.

Before submitting your affidavit, review the disputed account(s) with family members or friends who may have information about the account(s) or access to them.

Complete this affidavit as soon as possible. Many creditors ask that you send it within two weeks of receiving it. Delaying could slow the investigation.

Be as accurate and complete as possible. You *may* choose not to provide some of the information requested. However, incorrect or incomplete information will slow the process of investigating your claim and absolving the debt. Please print clearly.

When you have finished completing the affidavit, mail a copy to each creditor, bank or company that provided the thief with the unauthorized credit, goods or services you describe. Attach to each affidavit a copy of the Fraudulent Account Statement with information only on accounts opened at the institution receiving the packet, as well as any other supporting documentation you are able to provide.

Send the appropriate documents to each company by certified mail, return receipt requested, so you can prove that it was received. The companies will review your claim and send you a written response telling you the outcome of their investigation. **Keep a copy of everything you submit for your records.**

If you cannot complete the affidavit, a legal guardian or someone with power of attorney may complete it for you. Except as noted, the information you provide will be used only by the company to process your affidavit, investigate the events you report and help stop further fraud. If this affidavit is requested in a lawsuit, the company might have to provide it to the requesting party.

Completing this affidavit does not guarantee that the identity thief will be prosecuted or that the debt will be cleared.

If you haven't done so, report the fraud to the following organizations:

1. Each of the **three national consumer reporting agencies**. Ask each agency to place a "fraud alert" on your credit report, and send you a copy of your credit file. When you have completed your affidavit packet, you may want to send them a copy to help them investigate the disputed accounts.

- **Equifax Credit Information Services, Inc.** 1-(800) 525-6285 (Hearing impaired call 1-800-255-0056 and ask the operator to call the Auto Disclosure Line at 1-800-685-1111 to obtain a copy of your report.) PO Box 740241, Atlanta, GA 30374-0241 www.equifax.com

- **Experian Information Solutions, Inc.** 1-(888) 397-3742/TDD 1-(800)-972-0322, PO Box 9530, Allen, TX 75013. www.experian.com

- **TransUnion**, 1-(800)-680-7289/TDD 1-(877)-553-7803. Fraud Victim Assistance Division, PO Box 6790, Fullerton, CA 92634-6790 www.tuc.com

2. The **fraud department at each creditor, bank, or utility/service** that provided the identity thief with unauthorized credit, goods or services. This would be a good time to find out if the company accepts this affidavit, and whether they require notarization or a copy of the police report.

3. Your local **police department**. Ask the officer to take a report and give you the report number or a copy of the report. When you have completed the affidavit packet, you may want to give your police department a copy to help them add to their report and verify the crime.

4. The FTC, which maintains the Identity Theft Data Clearinghouse — the federal government's centralized identity theft complaint database — and provides information to identity theft victims. You can call toll-free **1-877-ID-THEFT (1-877-438-4338)**, visit **www.consumer.gov/idtheft** or send mail to:

Identity Theft Data Clearinghouse
Federal Trade Commission
600 Pennsylvania Avenue, NW
Washington, DC 20580

The FTC collects complaints from identity theft victims and shares their information with law enforcement nationwide. This information also may be shared with other government agencies, consumer reporting agencies, and companies where the fraud was perpetrated to help resolve identity theft related problems.

Appendix 2

Name Change States

In theory, a legal name change can be accomplished in all states. The reality is that some states make the process very difficult and require reams of personal information to be placed into the public record. The following states are easier for name changes, although a certain level of paperwork and formalities will need to be complied with.

Alabama	Indiana	Nebraska	Tennessee
Alaska	Kansas	Nevada	Texas
Arkansas	Kentucky	New Hampshire	Utah
California	Maryland	New Jersey	Washington
Colorado	Massachusetts	North Dakota	West Virginia
Delaware	Missouri	Ohio	Wisconsin
Idaho	Montana	South Carolina	Wyoming

Social Security Number Allocations

Since 1972, Social Security numbers have been issued by our central office. The first three (3) digits of a person's Social Security number are determined by the ZIP Code of the mailing address shown on the application for a Social Security number. Prior to 1972, Social Security numbers were assigned by our field offices. The number merely established that his/her card was issued by one of our offices in that State.

Area Group Serial

The Social Security number consists of nine (9) digits – 123 – 45 – 6789. The first three (3) digits denote the area (or State) where the application for an original Social Security number was filed.

Within each area, the group number (middle two (2) digits) range from 01 to 99 but are not assigned in consecutive order. For administrative reasons, group numbers issued first consist of the ODD numbers from 01 to 09 and then EVEN numbers from 10 through 98, within each area number allocated to a State. After all numbers in group 98 of a particular area have been issued, the EVEN Groups 02 through 08 are used, followed by ODD Groups 11 through 99.

Within each group, the serial numbers (last four (4) digits) run consecutively from 0001 through 9999.

This chart below shows how Group numbers are assigned:

ODD – 01, 03, 05, 07, 09 – EVEN – 10 to 98
EVEN – 02, 04, 06, 08 – ODD – 11 to 99

NOTE:

See the latest Social Security Number Monthly Issuance Table for the latest SSN area ranges issued to date. Alleged Social Security numbers containing area numbers other than those found on that table are impossible.

THIS DATA IS STRICTLY FOR INFORMATIONAL PURPOSES

****

The chart below shows the first 3 digits of the Social Security numbers assigned throughout the United States and its possessions.

001-003	New Hampshire	212-220	Maryland
004-007	Maine	221-222	Delaware
008-009	Vermont	223-231	Virginia
010-034	Massachusetts	691-699*	
035-039	Rhode Island	232-236	West Virginia
040-049	Connecticut	232	North Carolina
050-134	New York	237-246	
135-158	New Jersey	681-690*	
159-211	Pennsylvania	247-251	South Carolina

654-658		505-508	Nebraska
252-260	Georgia	509-515	Kansas
667-675		516-517	Montana
261-267	Florida	518-519	Idaho
589-595		520	Wyoming
268-302	Ohio	521-524	Colorado
303-317	Indiana	650-653*	
318-361	Illinois	525, 585	New Mexico
362-386	Michigan	648-649	
387-399	Wisconsin	526-527	Arizona
400-407	Kentucky	600-601	
408-415	Tennessee	528-529	Utah
756-763*		646-647	
416-424	Alabama	530	Nevada
425-428	Mississippi	680*	
587		531-539	Washington
588*		540-544	Oregon
752-755*		545-573	California
429-432	Arkansas	602-626	
676-679*		574	Alaska
433-439	Louisiana	575-576	Hawaii
659-665*		750-751*	
440-448	Oklahoma	577-579	District of Columbia
449-467	Texas	580	Virgin Islands
627-645		580-584	Puerto Rico
468-477	Minnesota	596-599	
478-485	Iowa	586	Guam
486-500	Missouri	586	American Samoa
501-502	North Dakota	586	Philippine Islands
503-504	South Dakota	700-728	Railroad Board**

Note: The same area, when shown more than once, means that certain numbers have been transferred from one state to another, or that an area has been divided for use among certain geographic locations.

Any number beginning with 000 will NEVER be a valid SSN.

The information in our records about an individual is confidential by law and cannot be disclosed except in certain very restricted cases permitted by regulations.

* = New areas allocated, but not yet issued
** 700-728 Issuance of these numbers to railroad employees was discontinued July 1, 1963.

Highest Group Issued as of 05/01/02

This list shows the SSN area and group numbers that are in the process of being issued as of May 1, 2002. Social Security numbers may also be viewed by State or Area.

001 96	002 96	003 96	004 04	005 02	006 02	007 02
008 86	009 84	010 86	011 86	012 86	013 86	014 84
015 84	016 84	017 84	018 84	019 84	020 84	021 84
022 84	023 84	024 84	025 84	026 84	027 84	028 84
029 84	030 84	031 84	032 84	033 84	034 84	035 68
036 68	037 68	038 68	039 66	040 04	041 04	042 04
043 04	044 04	045 04	046 02	047 02	048 02	049 02
050 92	052 92	053 92	054 92	055 92	056 92	057 92
058 92	059 92	060 92	061 92	062 90	063 90	064 90
065 90	066 90	067 90	068 90	069 90	070 90	071 90
072 90	073 90	074 90	075 90	076 90	077 90	078 90
079 90	080 90	081 90	082 90	083 90	084 90	085 90
086 90	087 90	088 90	089 90	090 90	091 90	092 90
093 90	094 90	095 90	096 90	097 90	098 90	099 90
100 90	101 90	102 90	103 90	104 90	105 90	106 90
107 90	108 90	109 90	110 90	111 90	112 90	113 90
114 90	115 90	116 90	117 90	118 90	119 90	120 90
121 90	122 90	123 90	124 90	125 90	126 90	127 90
128 90	129 90	130 90	131 90	132 90	133 90	134 90
135 11	136 11	137 11	138 11	139 11	140 11	141 11
142 11	143 11	144 08	145 08	146 08	147 08	148 08
149 08	150 08	151 08	152 08	153 08	154 08	155 08
156 08	157 08	158 08	159 80	160 80	161 80	162 80
163 80	164 80	165 80	166 80	167 80	167 80	168 80
169 80	170 80	171 80	172 80	173 80	174 80	175 80
176 80	177 80	178 80	179 80	180 80	181 80	182 80
183 80	184 80	185 80	186 80	187 80	188 80	189 78
190 78	191 78	192 78	193 78	194 78	195 78	196 78
197 78	198 78	199 78	200 78	201 78	202 78	203 78
204 78	205 78	206 78	207 78	208 78	209 78	210 78
211 78	212 63	213 63	214 63	215 63	216 63	217 63
218 61	219 61	220 61	221 96	222 94	223 93	224 93
225 93	226 93	227 93	228 91	229 91	230 91	231 91
232 49	233 49	234 49	235 47	236 47	237 99	238 99
239 99	240 99	241 97	242 97	243 97	244 97	245 97
246 97	247 99	248 99	249 99	250 99	251 99	252 99
253 99	254 99	255 99	256 99	257 99	258 99	259 99
260 99	261 99	262 99	263 99	264 99	265 99	266 99
267 99	268 06	269 06	270 06	271 06	272 06	273 06
274 06	275 06	276 06	277 06	278 06	279 06	280 06

281 06	282 06	283 06	284 06	285 06	286 06	287 06
288 06	289 06	290 06	291 06	292 06	293 06	294 06
295 06	296 06	297 06	298 04	299 04	300 04	301 04
302 04	303 25	304 25	305 25	306 25	307 25	307 25
308 25	309 25	310 25	311 23	312 23	313 23	314 23
315 23	316 23	317 23	318 98	319 98	320 98	321 98
322 98	323 98	324 98	325 98	326 98	327 98	328 98
329 98	330 98	331 98	332 98	333 98	334 98	335 98
336 98	337 98	338 98	339 98	340 98	341 98	342 98
343 98	344 98	345 98	346 98	347 98	348 98	349 98
350 98	350 98	351 98	352 98	353 98	354 98	355 98
356 98	357 98	358 98	359 98	360 96	361 96	362 27
363 27	364 27	365 27	366 27	367 27	368 27	369 27
370 27	370 27	371 27	372 27	373 27	374 27	375 27
376 27	377 27	378 27	379 27	380 27	381 27	382 27
383 27	384 27	385 25	386 25	387 23	388 23	389 21
390 21	391 21	392 21	393 21	394 21	395 21	396 21
397 21	398 21	399 21	400 59	401 59	402 59	403 57
404 57	405 57	406 57	407 57	408 93	409 93	410 93
411 91	412 91	413 91	414 91	415 91	416 53	417 53
418 53	419 53	420 53	421 53	422 53	423 53	424 53
425 91	426 91	427 91	428 91	429 99	430 99	431 99
432 99	433 99	434 99	435 99	436 99	437 99	438 99
439 99	440 17	441 17	442 15	443 15	444 15	445 15
446 15	447 15	448 15	449 99	450 99	450 99	451 99
452 99	453 99	454 99	455 99	456 99	457 99	458 99
459 99	460 99	461 99	462 99	463 99	464 99	465 99
466 99	467 99	468 41	469 41	470 41	470 41	471 41
472 41	473 39	474 39	475 39	476 39	477 39	478 31
479 31	480 31	481 31	482 31	483 31	484 31	485 29
486 19	487 19	488 19	489 19	490 19	491 19	492 19
493 17	494 17	495 17	496 17	497 17	498 17	499 17
500 17	501 27	502 27	503 33	504 33	505 45	506 43
507 43	508 43	509 21	510 21	511 21	512 19	513 19
514 19	515 19	516 37	517 35	518 63	519 63	520 43
521 99	522 99	523 99	524 99	525 99	526 99	527 99
528 99	529 99	530 99	531 49	532 49	533 49	534 49
535 49	536 49	537 47	538 47	539 47	540 61	541 61
542 61	543 61	544 61	545 99	546 99	547 99	548 99
549 99	550 99	551 99	552 99	553 99	554 99	555 99
556 99	557 99	558 99	559 99	560 99	561 99	562 99
563 99	564 99	565 99	566 99	567 99	568 99	569 99
570 99	571 99	572 99	573 99	574 35	575 93	576 91
577 33	578 33	579 33	580 35	581 99	582 99	583 99
584 99	585 99	586 49	587 89	589 99	590 99	591 99
592 99	593 99	594 99	595 99	596 70	597 70	598 68
599 68	600 99	601 99	602 33	603 31	604 31	605 31

606 31	607 31	608 31	609 31	610 31	611 31	612 31
613 31	614 31	615 31	616 31	617 31	618 31	619 31
620 31	621 31	622 31	623 31	624 31	625 31	626 31
627 80	628 80	629 80	630 80	631 80	632 80	633 80
634 80	635 80	636 80	637 80	638 80	639 80	640 80
641 80	642 80	643 80	644 80	645 80	646 64	647 64
648 28	649 26	650 22	651 22	652 22	653 20	654 12
655 12	656 12	657 12	658 10	659 05	660 05	661 05
661 05	662 05	663 05	664 03	665 03	667 14	668 14
669 14	670 14	671 14	672 14	673 14	674 14	675 14
676 03	677 03	678 01	679 01	680 38	700 18	701 18
702 18	703 18	704 18	705 18	706 18	707 18	708 18
709 18	710 18	711 18	712 18	713 18	714 18	715 18
716 18	717 18	718 18	719 18	720 18	721 18	722 18
723 18	724 28	725 18	726 18	727 10	728 14	764 18
765 18	766 10	767 10	768 10	769 10	770 09	771 09
772 09						

Information Brokers

The following is a list of typical information brokers. This is not a recommendation, and information broker web sites should be consulted before ordering any searches. Additional information brokerage firms can be found by entering "information broker" or a similar term into any Internet search engine.

Docusearch.com
1077 Harbour Springs
Boca Raton, FL 33428
http://www.docusearch.com

USSearch.com
5401 Beethoven Street
Los Angeles, CA 90066
800-877-2410
fax: 310-822-7898
http://1800ussearch.com

SSN Trace/Find People Fast
PO Box 20190
St. Louis, MO 63123

US Trace.com
15413 Hall Road, Suite 211
Macomb, MI 48044

Must Know Checklist

The following information, at a minimum, should be committed to memory about the city or region that you are claiming as your new background.

- ☐ Size of city
- ☐ General layout and organization of the metro area
- ☐ Major industries
- ☐ Local specialities in food, culture, and recreation
- ☐ Name of pro and college sports teams
- ☐ Ethnic makeup of the area
- ☐ Major tourist/scenic sites
- ☐ Name of the Mayor
- ☐ Major recent current events
- ☐ Major events of historical importance
- ☐ Cost of living information
- ☐ Names of major retailers — grocery store chains, etc.
- ☐ Area codes and zip codes

Appendix 3

Incorporation Advertisement

WHY INCORPORATE?

Its the safest way to operate your business.
It is the lowest cost insurance you can buy for protection of your personal assets.

You heard about the woman who spilled hot coffee on herself and then sued McDonalds, and was awarded $180,000? Maybe McDonalds can afford it, but can you? Unplanned events happen.

● **Limit your liability**
Personal assets cannot be targets for creditors. Your home, car, savings will always remain untouched if you operate under the protection of the corporate umbrella.

● **Improve your tax picture**
Many benefits become fully deductible. Mixture of salary and dividends can minimize your taxes. In some situations, an S Corporation is the best choice because it prevents double taxation.

● **Privacy**
Ownership can be concealed from the public.

● **Stature**
Corporate image presents stronger marketing opportunities and improves access to financial sources.

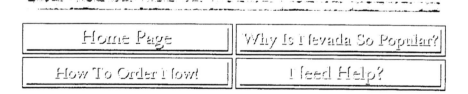

Home Page	Why Is Nevada So Popular?
How To Order Now!	I Need Help?

Frequently Asked Questions

The following information is based upon our experience and is accurate to the best of our knowledge. However, legal validity is not guaranteed.

Do I have to be a resident of the state?
No. In fact you do not have to be a U.S. citizen.

Do I have to be located in the state?
No. You never have to set foot in the state. If you are not physically present in the state, you must have a resident agent.

What is a resident agent?
It is someone or a corporation with offices in the state who can act as your agent for acceptance of legal service. The resident agent is the Secretary of State's recognized contact for your corporation. You must have a resident agent if you have no physical presence in the state of incorporation. Conversely, you do not need one if you do have a physical presence in that state. Corporation Makers includes a full year of resident agent service for all of its' clients as part of the incorporation package.

Can I conduct business in other states?
Yes. But you must comply with local laws and licensing of the state in which you do business.

What is a foreign corporation?
Any corporation doing business in a state other than the one it incorporated in is a foreign corporation (to that state). As such, you would register with the secretary of that state. Fees are usually involved.

I conduct business in many states, do I need to register with each one?
This is tricky. If you actually transact business in that state then you need to register. If you are merely promoting your business in that state then you probably do not have to register. One rule of thumb is: where do you take customer orders. In most instances, if you do not have any active and regular operations in the state, then you do not need to register as a foreign corporation. If you have doubts, you should get a legal opinion.

Where can I have bank accounts?
Anywhere. You can open up your corporate account in virtually any bank by providing the proper documents. Normally these include, Articles, Federal ID, Board Resolution, and good I.D. of the account signatories.

What does it cost to incorporate?
Very little with Corporation Makers. Costs include 1)state fees, 2)kit fees, 3)resident agent fees, and 4)service charges. So don't be fooled by those $25 and $45 catch your eye quotes from some of our competitors. They are misleading and inaccurate. Your best defense in understanding the true cost is to get to the bottom line. What will you be paying for the entire

package. Corporation Makers is lowest--Guaranteed. In case you are wondering, we charge $369 for a Nevada corporation (no kit), and $449 with a very handsome kit. These fees include the new Nevada filing fees effective August 1, 2001.

Why is Nevada so popular as a corporate haven?

Many reasons. Nevada does not disclose ownership. Unless you go public, no one will know who the shareholders are. Nevada has no state income tax. Nevada is the only state that does not have an information exchange agreement with the IRS. One person can incorporate and hold all offices. Annual fees are among the lowest in the nation. Meetings and activities do not have to be held in the state. A Nevada corporation can own other corporations, real estate, and stock. The State of Nevada is friendly to business and minimizes taxes, regulations, and oversight. You just can't find it any better.

Can my business in my home state be owned by a Nevada corporation?

Yes. Beautiful idea. Your accountant can establish methods for making your home business less profitable to the benefit of your Nevada corporation where taxes are lower.

Is it difficult to operate as a corporation?

No. We make it easy for you. You do have to document key events and you must have an annual meeting. Even if you are a one person corporation. Just follow our standard minutes and modify them to meet your situation. It takes a few minutes but it is extremely important that you behave like a corporation.

Can I use personal assets in my corporation?

Careful here. You can give, loan or rent them but you must document the transaction. In essence you can be a supplier of services. Do not commingle your bank accounts however. Keep money separate or you could offer creditors the same benefit of access to your funds. Rule of thumb. You are incorporating for certain benefits, among them liability limitation. So keep your stuff separate from the corporations "stuff".

Can my corporation operate out of my home?

Yes. You still need to comply with local law and restrictions about that. But you can rent space and equipment to your corporation.

Are corporate officers a matter of public record?

Yes. Names and addresses are filed with the state and are therefore available to anyone. Nevada requires this filing annually. They do not require notification of intervening changes. (Get the picture?). Other states may have the same requirement.

Can one person hold all offices?

Yes. In Nevada the same person can be president, treasurer, secretary, and director.

How many directors are required?

One in Nevada. Three in California unless the number of shareholders are fewer.

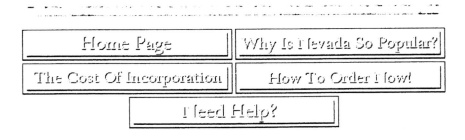

Home Page | Why Is Nevada So Popular?
The Cost Of Incorporation | How To Order Now!
I Need Help?

Course Credit by Examination from Ohio University

Enrollment Application
1-800-444-2910

Note: You must complete all information below. If information is missing or incomplete, your application cannot be processed and will be returned to you.

SSN: _____ Birthdate: M M _____ / D D _____ / Y Y _____ Gender M☐ F☐

Last Name: _____ Maiden: _____

First Name: _____ Middle: _____

Mailing Address _____

City _____ State _____ Zip Code _____

Telephone _____ E-mail Address _____

Ohio Resident ☐Y ☐N If yes, County _____

U.S. Citizen ☐Y ☐N If no, country of citizenship _____

Occupation _____ Are you presently enrolled at any Ohio University campus? ☐Y ☐N

Have you earned credit for any course (1) at any Ohio University or (2) through Independent Study? If so, give your:

College _____ Campus _____ Class Standing _____
 (Arts & Sciences, Business, etc.)   (Athens, Chillicothe, etc.)   (Fr, Soph, Jr, Sr)

Course Type (IS, WWW, ISP, CCE)	Dept.	Course No.	Course Title	*Replacement Credit? Y/N	Credit Hrs.	Study Guide Code (office use only)

*Are you enrolling in the course(s) to replace a previous grade from Ohio University? If so, please indicate "Y" for the course(s) in the appropriate column above. **Ohio University students must secure permission slips from their academic deans to enroll in Independent Study.** Permission slips are available in your college offices.

(Make check or money order payable to **Ohio University**. Students residing out of the United States should pay fees on a United States bank, payable in United States dollars. Bank drafts *will not* be accepted.)

Total Tuition (refer to course tuition listed with each course) $ _____

Other Charges (airmail, media fees, etc.) (Refer to airmail charges listed on page 13 of this catalog) $ _____

TOTAL $ _____

Method of Payment: ☐check or money order ☐Visa ☐MasterCard ☐Discover

Credit Card # ☐☐☐☐☐☐☐☐☐☐☐☐☐☐☐☐ Expiration Date ☐☐☐☐

Cardholder Signature _____

In signing this application, you are responsible for all policies in the current Ohio University Independent Study Bulletin.

Student's Signature _____ Date _____

Are you meeting a credit deadline (graduation, certification, etc.)? Y N If yes, what date? _____

Do you plan to apply for veteran's benefits? Y N If yes, have you provided proper documentation? Y N

(see Veteran's section under "Program Essentials," page 10.) Provide your VA Claim Number C– _____

Do you wish the pass/fail option? Y N Are you in the Ohio University External Student Program? Y N

Ways to Register: In person 🚶 By mail (see address on reverse side) 🚩 Internet Online 🌐 By fax (Credit card only, see Fax info on reverse side.)

Name

How Did You Learn About Independent Study?

A. Friend
B. Academic Advisor
C. Brochure, Mailer
D. Poster, Display
E. TV, Radio, Internet
F. Peterson's IS or Distance Learning Guides
G. Newspaper, Magazine (specify) _____
H. Other

Previous Education

☐ High School   9   10   11   12   Diploma   GED
☐ College   1   2   3   4   Degree _____
☐ Other Education _____

Purpose of Enrollment

A. College Entrance Requirement
B. Ohio University Student
C. Degree Credit Other Institution
D. Teacher Certification
E. Job Eligibility or Advancement
F. Personal Satisfaction
G. Other (specify) _____

Non-Ohio University Students Complete the Following

Are you presently enrolled at another school or college?   Y   N

Do you plan to use the credit at another institution?   Y   N

    If yes, where? _____

Are you a high school student?

(Note: If yes to any of the above questions, written permission from your academic dean, principal, or guidance counselor should be given below or sent by separate letter to the Independent Study office.)

_____

(Signature)   (Title)   (Institution)

Mail to: Enrollment Clerk   **Fax:** Enrollment Clerk   **Phone:** 1-800-444-2910
Independent Study   Independent Study
302 Tupper Hall, Ohio University   Ohio University
Athens, OH 45701-2979   (740) 593-2901

Independent and Distance Learning: **Course Enrollments**

Ohio

Courses by Correspondence

Course Information

- List of Courses
- Explanation of Media Icons
- Fees

How to Enroll

- Before you Enroll
- Courses Currently Unavailable
- Enrollment Application
- Ordering Textbooks

Disclaimer and Feedback

Lifelong Learning Programs

Our courses are developed by Ohio University faculty using the content of their classroom courses. A study guide helps you understand the material and contains assignments you submit to the instructor for evaluation and feedback. Your textbook and other print materials are often supplemented with audio or videotapes. You may enroll any time during the year, and you have one calendar year to complete a course.

Independent and Distance Learning correspondence courses provide a highly structured method of independent study involving a tutorial relationship with a faculty member who guides your learning and monitors your progress. **The detailed study guide, prepared by your instructor, provides an overview and the lesson units that direct you through the course**.

Most lessons require you to submit answers to objective questions or write brief essays or both. Some lessons may require a paper or project. The study guide often includes self-check tests that let you monitor your own progress. Generally, two supervised examinations are required--a midcourse and a final examination.

If you click on any course title in the IS or WEB course list, you will get a full page of information for that course.

Course Credit by Examination

Course Information

- List of Courses
- Explanation of media icons
- Fees

How to Enroll

- Before you Enroll
- Courses Currently
- Enrollement Application
- Ordering Textbooks

If you are familiar with a particular subject or are able to master content without assistance, you may be able to earn credit **through a single comprehensive examination**. You receive a course syllabus, obtain the textbook, and prepare for the examination without assistance from an instructor. As in courses by correspondence, you may enroll at any time, but you must take the examination within six months. Your grade on the examination becomes your grade for the course.

http://www.ohiou.edu/independent/islist.htm